COMAY

221.92
C728h

The Hebrew kings

DO NOT REMOVE BOOK CARD OR
DATE DUE SLIP, 15¢ CHARGE FOR
LOSS OR DAMAGE TO EITHER.

New Albany - Floyd County Public Library
New Albany, Indiana

NEW ALBANY-FLOYD COUNTY PUBLIC LIBRARY

3 3110 00140 5230

THE
HEBREW
KINGS

THE
HEBREW
KINGS

JOAN COMAY

WILLIAM MORROW AND COMPANY, INC.

NEW YORK   1977

Published in the United States in 1977.

Copyright © 1976 by Joan Comay

Published in Great Britain in 1976.

All rights reserved. No part of this book may be reproduced
or utilized in any form or by any means, electronic or
mechanical, including photocopying, recording or by any in-
formation storage and retrieval system, without permission
in writing from the Publisher. Inquiries should be addressed
to William Morrow and Company, Inc., 105 Madison Ave.,
New York, N. Y. 10016.

Printed in the United States of America.

Library of Congress Catalog Card Number 76-44606

ISBN 0-688-03139-0

1   2   3   4   5   6   7   8   9   10

Contents

Illustrations

1. Valley of Jezreel (*Ronald Sheridan*).
2. The Battle of Mount Gilboa, from the Winchester Bible (By kind permission of Canon Bussby).
3. *Samuel Appearing to Saul*; painting by Salvador Rosa; now in the Louvre, Paris (*Radio Times Hulton Picture Library*).
4. David's Jerusalem (*Ronald Sheridan*).
5. Pillar of Absalom (*Ronald Sheridan*).
6. David playing his harp (*Ronald Sheridan*).
7. Solomon deciding the fate of the child (*Mansell Collection*).
8. Solomon and Sheba; painting by Piero della Francesca; now in the church of San Francesco, Arezzo, Italy (*Mansell Collection*).
9. Samaria (*Ronald Sheridan*).
10. King Rehoboam: a detail from a fresco by Hans Holbein the Younger, *The Presumption of King Rehoboam*, 1530 (*Öffentliche Kunstsammlung, Basle*).
11. The Temple of Amon-Ra (*Ronald Sheridan*).
12. *Elijah Fed by The Ravens*, by Giovanni Girolamo Savoldo (*Samuel H. Kress Collection, National Gallery of Art, Washington DC*).
13. Elijah, Ahab and Jezebel, an engraving by Sherratt after T. M. Rooke (*Radio Times Hulton Picture Library*).
14. The Black Obelisk of Shalmaneser III, now in the British Museum (*Mansell Collection*).
15. Ivory artifact depicting woman seated on the throne (*Weidenfeld Archives*).
16. Excavations at Hazor (*Hebrew University, Jerusalem*).
17. The prophet Isaiah, by Bernardo di Pietro Ciuffagni; now in the cathedral at Florence, Italy (*Mansell Collection*).
18. Inscription from Hezekiah's tunnel, Jerusalem (*Ronald Sheridan*).
19. Stone wall relief from Sennacherib's palace, Nineveh; now in the British Museum (*British Museum*).
20. Siege of Jerusalem by Nebuchadnezzar (*Ronald Sheridan*).
21. Michelangelo's Jeremiah, a detail from the Sistine Chapel (*Radio Times Hulton Picture Library*).

Introduction

This book deals with the classic period of the Hebrew monarchy, from the accession of Saul at the end of the eleventh century BC to the Babylonian destruction of Jerusalem in 587 BC.

The United Monarchy of Saul, David and Solomon lasted just under a hundred years, and it split into two on Solomon's death. The two centuries of the northern kingdom of Israel saw frequent changes of regime, covering nineteen kings. The southern kingdom of Judah with its stable Davidic dynasty had twenty rulers in three hundred and fifty years. Altogether, therefore, the whole period included forty-two kings – to be precise, forty-one kings and one queen, Ataliah of Judah. They formed a remarkably diverse group ranging from illustrious monarchs like David and Solomon to obscure soldiers like Zimri or Shallum who usurped the northern throne by violent 'colonels' coups'.

The stage was the land of Canaan lying between the desert and the sea, which had been the Promised Land of the Israelites from the time of the patriarch Abraham about the eighteenth century BC. Under its succession of kings the small Hebrew nation struggled to survive against the pressures of its neighbours and the trampling cohorts of the imperial powers to the north and the south.

This was a time of courage and frailty accompanied by deathless spiritual achievement: the message of the classic prophets and the shaping of the Old Testament.

The main sources for the period are the Books of Samuel and Kings, supplemented by the parallel account in the Book of Chronicles compiled much later. It must be borne in mind that the Old Testament is a theological history rather than a political one. The biblical editors were less concerned with the survival of the state than with the survival of the faith. Occupants of the throne were rated good or bad according to the extent that they cherished or neglected the overriding covenant with

God, or that they resisted or yielded to the encroaching forces of paganism. The triumphs or disasters of the nation were rewards or punishments for its behaviour. It is in that broad framework of reference that the Bible tells the fascinating human stories of the Hebrew kings.

PART ONE

THE UNITED KINGDOM

1

The Judges

The great prophet Samuel lived and dispensed justice in the hill-top village of Ramah. It was in the tribal territory of Benjamin, ten kilometres north of the fortified Jebusite city of Jerusalem. Each year Samuel went on circuit to other Israelite towns within easy reach: Bethel, on the border of Ephraim; Gilgal, down in the Jordan valley; and Mizpeh just north of Ramah.

One day a deputation of tribal elders appeared before Samuel. There must have been much fearful discussion among them before they confronted the stern and formidable man of God with a demand they knew would arouse his wrath. 'Behold', they said to him, 'you are old and your sons do not walk in your ways; now appoint for us a king to govern us like all the nations.' (I Samuel 8:5)

The pointed reference to his two sons, Joel and Abijah, touched on Samuel's personal tragedy. He had obtained for them the position of local judges in Beersheba but they 'turned aside after gain; they took bribes and perverted justice'. (I Samuel 8:3)

The Prophet was dismayed by the demand of the elders. He warned them that a king would oppress and exploit them. Their sons would be taken as soldiers and their daughters as servants. Their best lands would be confiscated and tithes exacted from their crops and herds for the royal household.

His visitors stuck doggedly to their request. The Israelites were being oppressed or threatened by an external enemy, the Philistines, who had settled in the southern coastal plain of Canaan. The twelve tribes, loosely connected by ties of kinship and faith, were too weak and divided to withstand this pressure. They wanted a leader like 'all the nations' had. Stubbornly they repeated their demand to Samuel: 'Give us a king to govern us.' (I Samuel 8:6)

Hereditary kingship was indeed the prevailing system of government

3

in the Near East, from the powerful imperial potentates of Egypt, Babylonia, Assyria and the Hittites, to the leaders of the little Canaanite city-states, each consisting of a walled town with its surrounding villages and farms. Only the Israelites had never had an earthly ruler. When his grateful tribe offered to make Gideon king after he had routed the Midianite invaders, his reply exactly summed up the traditional Hebrew theocracy: 'I will not rule over you, and my son will not rule over you; the Lord will rule over you.' (Judges 8:23)

Two centuries had gone by since Moses had brought the Children of Israel out of Egypt, and Joshua had led them across the river Jordan into the Promised Land about 1225 BC. The wandering shepherds and herdsmen had settled down to a sedentary way of life as peasants and artisans, in hill-villages and small unwalled market towns. But much of the patriarchal nomad society had remained intact in the transition 'from the desert to the sown'.

THE TRIBAL SYSTEM

Each of the tribes claimed descent from one of the sons of Jacob (Israel) by his wives, the matriarchs Leah and Rachel, and their maids Zilpah and Bilhah. One of Jacob's twelve sons was Levi, the ancestor of a group that had no allotted territory but performed religious functions for the other tribes and was scattered among them. Two of the tribes, Manasseh and Ephraim, were named after sons of Joseph, that is, grandsons of Jacob – thus preserving the figure for the tribes of twelve, which seems to have had a mystic meaning for all the semitic peoples.

Within each tribe the basic unit was the *bet-av* (father's house). The head of the household had undisputed authority over his wives and concubines, his sons and their progeny, the servants, slaves and property belonging to the family.

A group of such households with a common ancestor formed a clan or sub-tribe. The heads of the clans, or a council selected from them, were the 'elders' of the tribe.

In the desert wandering this system based on kinship gave each tribe and sub-tribe internal cohesion, while the tribes accepted Moses, and after him Joshua, as their single leader.

The bonds shaped by the harsh needs of the desert became weaker in the settled conditions of Canaan. Landless families moved from one

4

tribal territory to another. Elements of the local population were absorbed. The authority of the elders was undermined when their clans became town-dwellers. Yet somehow the traditional tribal system adjusted itself to change, and leading heads of families and clans remained responsible for keeping order, settling disputes, and administering family law.

The tribes shared no central institutions – no common ruler, capital city, civil service, priesthood or army. 'In those days there was no king in Israel; every man did what was right in his own eyes.' (Judges 21:25) They were held together by ethnic ties, by shared traditions about their origin and past history, by a God and a faith unlike any others in the region, and by the pressures of hostile neighbours that compelled them to come to one another's help.

The Conquest had not been as swift or complete as the Book of Joshua suggests. The Book of Judges gives a different and probably truer picture of the settlement as a prolonged and difficult process. The Israelites managed to occupy mainly the sparsely populated hill areas of the country, where resources of land and water were meagre and subsistence was a daily struggle.

They did not have the strength or technical means to overrun the fertile and more densely populated maritime plain or the broad valleys that intersected the hills. The elders of Manasseh and Ephraim complained to Joshua that 'the hill country is not enough for us ...' (Joshua 17:16) He replied bluntly that as they were not strong enough to conquer the Canaanites in the Beth-shan and Jezreel valleys, they had to make more room for themselves by clearing patches of virgin soil among the boulders and woods that covered their hills.

The settlement was helped by two technological advances. One was the use of iron tools, introduced into Canaan by the Philistines, who jealously kept to themselves the craft of iron-smelting:

Now there was no smith to be found throughout all the land of Israel; for the Philistines said, 'Lest the Hebrews make themselves swords or spears;' but everyone of the Israelites went down to the Philistines to sharpen his plow-shares, his mattock, his axe or his sickle; and the charge was a pim for the plowshares and for the mattocks, and a third of a shekel for sharpening the axes and for setting the goads. [I Samuel. 13:19–21] [A pim was two-thirds of a shekel.]

The other key technique was the storage of water all the year round in rock-hewn cisterns, lined with whitewashed plaster. This made it possible for the settlers to move away from the few natural springs, in spite of the rainless summer.

The Israelite settlement covered several areas. East of the Jordan valley and the Dead Sea were Reuben in the south, Gad in the centre and half the tribe of Manasseh in the north, in Gilead. The tribe of Reuben remained semi-nomadic, and its identity became blurred during the period of the Judges.

In the northern part of the country Asher was allotted western Galilee, Naphtali and Zebulun central and eastern Galilee, and Issachar the eastern part of the Jezreel valley. These tribes did not gain a footing in the plains but remained in the highlands, hemmed in by the Canaanites along the coast and Canaanite strongholds like Megiddo and Beth-shan, which commanded the Jezreel Valley.

The Galilee tribes were thus separated from the central hill-region, occupied by the 'Joseph' tribes of Ephraim and half of Manasseh.

Benjamin's portion was a narrow belt of hill-country just north of Jerusalem. Dan was at first located in the foothills and coastal plain west of Benjamin; but it was a struggle to hold that territory against Philistine pressure, and most of the tribe later migrated to the extreme north-east corner of the country, near the sources of the Jordan river.

The Hebron hills to the south of Jerusalem and the northern Negev belonged to the tribes of Judah and Simeon. Within this territory, round Beersheba, the tribe of Simeon continued a semi-nomadic way of life and was in due course absorbed into Judah.

Between Judah and the tribes farther north lay a line of Canaanite fortified cities and outposts, from Jerusalem to Gezer on the coastal plain. Elsewhere within the Israelite territory there were more Canaanite enclaves that were not subdued until a later stage.

During the twelfth and eleventh centuries BC, the period covered by the Book of Judges, each of the Israelite tribes was from time to time involved in local wars against hostile neighbours or bands of desert raiders. In the Old Testament the history of the Hebrew people is usually interpreted in terms of its relations with the Lord. The opening chapters of the Book of Judges explain that when the Israelites came under attack they were being punished for religious backsliding:

And the people of Israel did what was evil in the sight of the Lord and served the Baals; . . . they went after other gods, from among the gods of the peoples who were round about them, and bowed down to them; . . . So the anger of the Lord was kindled against Israel, and he gave them over to plunderers, who plundered them; and he sold them into the power of their enemies round about . . . and they were in sore straits. [Judges 2:11–15]

This theme would later run right through the story of the Hebrew kings.

The fact that so many small kingdoms and city-states in Canaan remained unconquered by the Israelites was presented as part of the divine plan to hold them in the path of righteousness. 'I will not henceforth drive out before them any of the nations that Joshua left when he died, that by them I may test Israel, whether they will take care to walk in the way of the Lord as their fathers did, or not.' (Judges 2:21–2)

Some scholars divide the non-Israelite population of the country into two main ethnic and cultural groups: the Canaanites and the Amorites. The latter (referred to in Egyptian sources as Amurru) seem to have moved down from Syria and Lebanon about the time of the Israelite invasion, and to have established a line of kingdoms east of the Jordan: Bashan, Geshur, Ammon, Moab and Edom. They also penetrated the hill areas of Canaan, west of the Jordan, and the 'Perizzites, Hivites and Jebusites' mentioned in the Bible (for instance, in Judges 3:5) were probably of Amorite stock.

The most advanced of the Canaanite peoples were the Phoenicians, along what is now the Lebanese coast. Their ships and traders sailed the length of the Mediterranean and established a series of colonies and trading posts.

About the twelfth century, after Joshua's time, the Philistines appeared in the southern coastal plain of Canaan. They were newcomers to the region, a branch of the Sea Peoples whose galleys pushed from the Aegean Sea across the eastern Mediterranean. They penetrated the Hittite empire in Asia Minor and harassed the coast of Egypt – much as the Norsemen and Danes were to do in the North Sea in a later age. The Philistine settlers in Canaan established five city-states – Gaza, Ashdod, Ashkelon, Ekron and Gath – each under its own king or *seren*, but joined together in a league.

Canaan lay in the path of the mighty empires that rose and fell in the fertile valley of the Nile to the south and the Mesopotamian river-basin of the Tigris and the Euphrates to the north-east. The small peoples in Canaan enjoyed independence only when one wave of conquest had receded and another not yet taken its place. The period of the Judges was such an interlude. Three centuries of Egyptian colonial rule had ended before Joshua crossed the Jordan. The expansion southward of the Hittites, a warrior people originating in Anatolia, had been blocked in the thirteenth century by the Pharaoh Rameses II of Egypt; soon after, Hatti (the Hittite empire), disintegrated under the blows of the Sea Peoples. In Mesopotamia Assyrian power was rising but it would be centuries before the Assyrian cohorts rolled westward to the sea. During these years Canaan lay in a no man's land between the Great Powers of the ancient Near East. It was against their local neighbours in Canaan that the Israelite tribes struggled to survive.

THE JUDGES

In times of trouble the tribal elders would turn to some individual to lead them in battle, in the belief that the 'spirit of the Lord' had entered into him for the purpose. 'Then the Lord raised up judges, who saved them out of the power of those who plundered them.' (Judges 2:16) The word 'Judges' (Hebrew *Shoftim*) may be misleading. They were not judicial officers; their function was to rally the men of their tribe, or a group of tribes, against an enemy that threatened them. When the crisis passed, their task was done – although they may have continued to exercise influence in tribal matters and settle disputes. The Hebrew Judges have been called 'charismatic' leaders, a term derived from an ancient Greek word meaning a special grace bestowed upon a mortal by the gods. This kind of spontaneous and temporary leadership in an emergency bore no resemblance to the dynastic monarchies of the surrounding nations.

The Book of Judges relates seven such major crises. Five 'minor' Judges also get brief mention: Tola in Issachar; Jair in Gilead; Ibzan in Judah; Elon in Zebulun; and Abdon in Ephraim. They were apparently important clan heads and men of property, exercising authority in their respective towns; but there is no indication that they led campaigns against external foes. They may have been mentioned by later biblical editors to bring the number of Judges up to twelve, matching the number of tribes.

Othniel is the earliest of the Judges. Belonging to the tribe of Judah, he is first mentioned as a nephew of Joshua's lieutenant Caleb, and as having captured the Canaanite town of Debir, south-west of Hebron, during the Conquest. The Book of Judges states cryptically that Othniel later delivered his people from oppression by 'Cushan-rishathaim, king of Mesopotamia'. The identity of this ruler or his actual country remains unknown.

Ehud was of the tribe of Benjamin. The part of its territory that lay in the Jordan valley had been occupied by Eglon, the fat king of Moab. Ehud stabbed him to death, then rallied his tribesmen to drive the Moabites back across the river.

Shamgar, the son of Anath, is stated in a single sentence to have killed six hundred Philistines with an ox-goad. No clue is given about his period or tribe, and some biblical scholars have expressed doubt as to whether he was an Israelite at all.

Deborah the prophetess rallied the central and northern tribes to break the domination of that part of the country by an alliance of Canaanite kings. She prevailed upon Barak from the tribe of Naphtali to lead the Israelite forces, and they routed the Canaanite chariot troops in the battle of Mount Tabor in the Jezreel valley. This victory was of great strategic importance since the Israelite tribes in the Galilee highlands could now link up with those in the hills of Ephraim. According to the prose account of the battle only the tribes of Naphtali and Zebulun took part in it. However the Song of Deborah indicates that she issued a general mobilization call, and that contingents were also sent from her tribe of Issachar, from Ephraim and Benjamin, and from the sub-tribe of Manasseh in Gilead, east of the Jordan. Deborah praises those who responded and pours her anger on those who hung back – Gad, Dan, Asher and Reuben. It is interesting that there is no mention of the southern tribes, Judah and Simeon – an early sign of the gulf that would later split the Hebrew nation into two small rival kingdoms.

The war of Gideon, from the tribe of Manasseh, was waged against the camel-riding Midianites that had moved into the Jezreel valley with their flocks and their bedouin tents. Gideon's famous night attack at the spring of Ain Harod, in the tribal territory of Issachar, panicked the enemy into flight. He chased the Midianites across the river fords and over three hundred kilometres into the desert, and slew their chieftains.

Gideon's son, Abimelech, launched a three-year experiment in kingship after his father's death – the only one of its kind in the period of the Judges. At first he based himself on the Canaanite inhabitants of Shechem (Nablus), his mother's community, and disposed of any potential rivals by murdering his brothers. Jotham the youngest escaped. In crying out to the citizens of Shechem from the top of Mount Gerizim, he told them the parable of the trees that sought a king. The olive tree, the fig tree and the vine in turn declined the honour, pleading that they preferred to go on producing fruits that brought good to gods and men. Only the bramble accepted, but warned that a fire would come out of it and consume those who anointed it king. Jotham's dire prediction came true. When the men of Shechem turned against Abimelech, he destroyed the city and its pagan temple. (Archaeological evidence bears out that Shechem was in fact razed about that time.) Abimelech himself came to an undignified end soon after. While he was taking a Canaanite town near Shechem, a woman dropped a millstone on to his head from the tower wall and crushed his skull.

The story of Jephthah concerned the pressure on his native Gilead from the adjacent Trans-jordan kingdom of Ammon. The outcast son of a harlot, he became the daring leader of a robber band, and was then invited back to take command of the Israelite forces. In fulfilment of a vow to God before the battle, he was tragically impelled to sacrifice his only daughter when he returned home. After delivering his tribe from the Ammonite foe, Jephthah was caught up in an unpleasant inter-tribal conflict with the men of Ephraim, who had crossed into Gilead and were trapped at the river fords on their way back.

Samson the Danite was a strange figure to be included in the roster of the Judges. He was not a tribal leader but a legendary and rather boisterous folk-hero. His encounters with the Philistines show that they were pushing at that time into the Shefelah, the foothills of the Judean range. Betrayed by the Philistine woman Delilah, the blinded and captive Samson met a noble end by pulling down the temple of Dagon in Gaza on to his tormentors and himself.

The prophet Samuel, 'the Kingmaker', was the last and most influential of the Judges and the transitional figure between the tribal system and the monarchy. By his time, the second half of the eleventh century BC, the Philistines had become the major threat to the independence of the Israelite tribes. Samuel was a youth serving in the central sanctuary at Shiloh, half-way between Jerusalem and Shechem, when the Israelites were crushingly defeated by the Philistines in a battle near Aphek, on the edge of the coastal plain. To make matters worse, the sacred Ark of the Covenant kept at Shiloh had been sent to the battleground to inspire the Israelite fighters, and had fallen into Philistine hands. When a runner brought the fearful tidings, the aged high priest Eli fell backwards with shock and died of a broken neck. Soon after Shiloh was destroyed by the Philistine troops advancing into the hills.

When the elders came to Samuel and asked for a king, the Philistines were the established overlords of the central hill area of Ephraim and Benjamin. They maintained permanent garrisons in strategic towns and exacted tribute. Yet it was no easy matter for them to keep control of the hostile Israelite population. Communications were poor, the hill terrain was unsuited for the deployment of their formidable chariot forces and their isolated outposts were vulnerable to attack. At one point Samuel called together an assembly of tribesmen at Mizpah, eight kilometres north-west of Jerusalem, and conducted religious ceremonies to gain the Lord's help. A Philistine contingent coming up to the gathering was routed and chased back into the plain. This local victory was heartening, but gave only temporary respite. It was clear that subjection to the Philistines could be ended only if the tribes accepted a common leader.

The choice fell upon Saul, whose father Kish was a respected man of Gibeah in the tribe of Benjamin. Saul certainly looked the part – he was singularly handsome, and in a crowd towered head and shoulders above everyone else.

2

Saul

The Book of Samuel contains at least two interwoven accounts of Saul's election as king. In the first, Saul's father had sent the young man with a servant to find three she-asses that had strayed. The search took them on foot across a large stretch of hill-country, and they stayed away so long that Saul wanted to turn back 'lest my father cease to care about the asses and become anxious about us'. (I Samuel 9:5) They reached the town of Zuph, and heard that the respected seer Samuel had come there to preside over a sacrificial feast at the local hill-shrine or 'high place'. Saul accepted the servant's advice to consult the holy man about their search. The previous day, the Lord had revealed to the prophet Samuel that a Benjaminite would come to him, 'and you shall anoint him to be prince over my people Israel. He shall save my people from the hands of the Philistines . . .' (I Samuel 9:16) Unaware of this, Saul was astonished at the way Samuel received him, allotting him a place of honour and the choicest portion at the feast, and inviting him to sleep on the rooftop of the house where Samuel was staying.

Early next morning Samuel told Saul that he need not worry about the asses as they had been found. The prophet then disclosed the high destiny marked out for Saul and solemnly anointed his head from a vial of oil. On his way home Saul encountered 'a band of prophets coming down from the high place with harp, tambourine, flutes and lyre before them, prophesying'. (I Samuel 10:5) In their company Saul underwent a profound spiritual experience and emerged a changed man. That episode, says the Bible, was the origin of the proverbial expression 'is Saul also among the prophets?' – referring to someone who finds religion to the surprise of his friends.

Apparently these 'prophets' were part of a revivalist movement among the Israelites at the time. They formed wandering groups that worked themselves into religious ecstasy with the help of music, chanting and rhythmic dance. Their activities had patriotic as well as religious overtones, and no doubt helped to maintain the spirit of a people under subjection. Saul's brief immersion in their prophetic frenzy, when 'the spirit of God came mightily upon him . . .' (I Samuel 10:10), served as a religious initiation for the future king. As such it is given a prominent place in the narrative.

Back home, Saul told his family only that he had gone to Samuel about the missing asses, and kept quiet about 'the matter of the kingdom'.

There follows a different version of Saul's election. Samuel called together a rally of the tribes at Mizpah and carried out the ceremonial act of selecting a king by the drawing of lots. By this means the choice was narrowed down to the tribe of Benjamin, then to the clan of the Matrites, and finally to Saul, the son of Kish, as an individual member of that clan. There was some consternation when the nominee was not seen among those present. Found modestly hanging back with the equipment, he was brought forward and acclaimed by Samuel, and all the people shouted, 'Long live the king!'

In the ensuing chapter the narrative seems to jump back to an earlier course of events. Saul had been ploughing with oxen in his father's fields. He returned home to find the townsfolk in distress. Messengers from the Israelite town of Jabesh-gilead in Trans-jordan had come to seek help. Their town was under attack by Nahash, king of Ammon and was in desperate plight. It had sought to negotiate surrender terms, but the arrogant Ammonite ruler had declared he would put out the right eyes of all the men if they fell into his hands. 'And the spirit of God came mightily upon Saul when he heard these words and his anger was greatly kindled.' (I Samuel 11:6) He despatched messengers through the tribal areas with pieces of slain oxen, the traditional rallying cry to arms. By the following morning he had reached the scene of battle with a large volunteer force. He immediately attacked the Ammonite camp and routed the enemy. After this victory Samuel summoned the people to Gilgal in the Jordan valley, where Saul was formally confirmed as king, with sacrifices and public rejoicing.

This narrative is quite consistent with the earlier story of Saul's meeting with Samuel at Zuph when he was looking for his father's asses. At that time Samuel's anointing of Saul had remained a private matter between them, and Saul had gone back to resume his normal life in his father's household. The relief of Jabesh-gilead gave Saul a chance to prove himself as a battle leader, and it was only then that his election as king was publicly fulfilled. This sequence was logical. What the hour needed was not a change of political system, but a commander-in-chief who would unify the tribes in a war of liberation from the Philistines. Saul's role was a projection of the charismatic leaders that had arisen during the period of the Judges, when the survival of their tribes was threatened. During his reign he was almost wholly occupied with military campaigns, within the general framework of the tribal confederacy. It was only under Saul's successor, David, and even more so under Solomon, that the monarchy was developed into a strongly organized instrument of central rule.

The accounts of Saul's election reflect not only different factual narratives, but also conflicting attitudes to the institution of monarchy. Certain passages are marked by a strong anti-royalist sentiment and the acceptance of a king is regarded as at best a necessary evil. When Samuel consulted the Lord concerning the demand of the elders, the divine assent could hardly have been more grudging and reproachful. 'Hearken to the voice of the people in all that they say to you; for they have not rejected you but they have rejected me from being king over them . . . you shall solemnly warn them, and show them the ways of the king who shall reign over them.' (I Samuel 8:7, 9) This is just what Samuel proceeded to do, explaining to the elders that kings exploited their subjects. The same resentful note recurs in the accounts of the king-making ceremonies at Mizpah and at Gilgal. Samuel grimly warned the people that their paramount duty remained obedience to the Lord's commandments – and, by implication, to Samuel as the Lord's spokesman: '. . . if you still do wickedly, you shall be swept away, both you and your king'. (I Samuel 12:25) These utterances have an ominous ring in the light of the bitter antagonism that Samuel would later display towards Saul.

Mixed with such passages are others favourable to the idea of kingship. This is so throughout the story of Saul's private anointing by Samuel at Zuph. In instructing Samuel to perform this act, the Lord explains that Saul will be the saviour and ruler of his people with divine sanction. Samuel carries out his part with great willingness. In the whole of this passage there is no hint of disapproval.

How does it come about that a favourable opinion of kingship and a sour distaste for it can mingle in the same chapters of the Bible? It must be remembered that the Old Testament is an anthology compiled and edited over a thousand years (roughly from the tenth century BC to the first century AD) and that the written sources were derived from much older oral traditions. During this lengthy process the text was coloured by changing ideas in different periods.

In the Book of Samuel, much of the text was based on a chronicle believed to have been written in Solomon's reign by one of his senior officials, who was able to draw on the palace archives. It is known to bible scholars as the Early Source. For an official history this document is remarkably objective, and does not gloss over the human weaknesses or the less attractive episodes in the careers of the two soldier-kings, Saul and David. But its basic premise is that the monarchy is God-ordained, and serves as the divine instrument for the salvation and guidance of His chosen people.

The so-called Later Source in the Book of Samuel dates from about 750–650 BC, the century that saw the decline and fall of the northern kingdom of Israel and Assyrian domination of the southern kingdom of Judah. By then the institution of kingship had become tarnished in Israelite eyes. That was the era of the classical Hebrew prophets. Much of their utterances and writings had an anti-establishment slant, and they did not hesitate to censure royal behaviour. The thunderous thesis of the prophets was that no kings or armies could save the kingdom, but only a return to the ways of God.

In its final form the Book of Samuel is an amalgam of both attitudes: the pro-royalist and the anti-royalist.

THE WARRIOR-KING (1020–1000 BC?)

Saul remained in his home town of Gibeah, and it became the royal seat. By later standards it was a modest and unpretentious capital, situated on a hill-top five kilometres north of Jerusalem. Here at Tel-el-Ful (the modern Arabic name), the archaeologists' spade has dug up the foundations of a rectangular citadel of rough stone blocks. It is believed to have served Saul as both fortress and residence – the word 'palace' sounds grand for such a simple structure. Three thousand years later, during the Jordanian occupation of East Jerusalem from 1948 to 1967, King Hussein started building himself a summer palace on the same site. It was left incomplete when the area was occupied by Israel in the Six-Day War, and remains a skeleton on the ridge to the right of the Jerusalem–Ramallah highway.

Since the relevant verses are mutilated, it is uncertain how old Saul was when he became king, or how long he reigned. At the outset he appears in the narrative as a young man. But he became king as a married man with three sons and two daughters, and the eldest son Jonathan was old enough to serve under his father as a battle commander. The length of his reign may have been about twenty years.

Saul soon launched an armed rebellion against the Philistines – the primary purpose for which he had been elected. He organized a force of three thousand fighting men, divided into three regiments. One regiment of a thousand men led by Jonathan was mustered in Gibeah while Saul held the remainder in reserve. Jonathan's task force then attacked and overran the Philistine garrison in the nearby hill-town of Geba. This success was only the opening blow in a war that would outlast Saul. But it resounded throughout the Israelite tribes. The king sent out a general mobilization call for the tribesmen to join him at Gilgal in the Jordan valley.

The Philistines reacted at once to this challenge. A powerful army of horsemen, chariot troops and infantry advanced across the hills of Benjamin and occupied the strategic town of Michmash on the edge of the Judean escarpment, eleven kilometres north of Jerusalem. It looked down into the deep gorge known in modern times by the Arabic name of Wadi es-Suwenit. At this display of strength most of Saul's hurriedly recruited forces melted away in disorder, hiding in caves or fleeing across the fords of the Jordan. Saul was left with a hard core of six hundred men, poorly armed since they were still unable to make iron weapons for themselves: 'So on the day of the battle there was neither sword nor spear found in the hand of any of the people with Saul and Jonathan, but Saul and his son Jonathan had them.' (I Samuel 13:22)

There now occurred the first open clash between the king and his prophetic patron. Saul had been told to wait seven days at Gilgal for Samuel, who would offer up the sacrifices customary at the beginning of a campaign. When the time passed without the prophet's arrival, and his own forces were disintegrating, Saul made the burnt offerings himself. Samuel appeared and bitterly rebuked the king, without explaining his own delay. There were doubtless two reasons for the old man's fury. Instead of remaining a docile instrument, the king had acted on his own judgement. What was worse, Saul had performed a religious act, thereby encroaching on Samuel's domain. The estrangement between the two leaders, the secular and the spiritual, would not be healed again.

Saul moved his small force up the escarpment to Geba, facing the enemy camp at Michmash with the deep ravine between them. The main Philistine body sent out columns in three directions to consolidate their hold on the countryside. Jonathan turned the tide by an unauthorized act of daring. Without asking the king's permission, he slipped away with his armour-bearer. They climbed down into the wadi, scaled the cliff on the other side and took by surprise a party of Philistine soldiers at the top. This sudden assault from a totally unexpected quarter caused confusion and panic in the camp. Puzzled by the signs of turmoil, Saul had a roll-call taken of his own men and discovered that Jonathan and one other were missing. The king decided to advance and attack. The Philistines started to flee westward and were pursued by an Israelite force rapidly swelling with recruits. The remnants of the enemy streamed through the vale of Ajalon and reached the safety of the coastal plain.

On the day of battle Saul had commanded his men to observe a rigid fast, on penalty of death. No clear explanation is offered for this seemingly irrational order which reduced the stamina of the soldiers. Saul may have suffered from a sense of guilt after Samuel's attack on him at Gilgal, and sought by the fast to regain the Lord's goodwill. He was dumbfounded to discover that Jonathan, in ignorance of the order, had broken the fast by eating some wild honey. Saul yielded to the appeal of the soldiers, and spared his son, who had been the hero of the day.

Jonathan was found to be the guilty person through invoking the Urim and Thummim, a sacred device for divining, probably by taking lots. Except that they were carried in the breastplate of the chief priest, no knowledge has survived about the nature of the Urim and Thummim. This passage is the only reference in the Bible to their actual use in a specific situation.

Saul was given further cause that day to fear the Lord's displeasure. After the battle his hungry men promptly slew and ate livestock captured as booty, without first draining the blood as prescribed. As soon as he heard this Saul constructed a rough altar of stone and had the remaining animals brought to it for ritual slaughter.

By the victory at Michmash, the central hill-country was liberated from the Philistine yoke, and the threat had receded for the time being. It would revive again in the latter part of Saul's reign, with disastrous consequences for his kingdom and himself. Meanwhile he could turn his attention to other hostile neighbours to the east and the south. They included the kingdoms of Ammon, Moab and Edom on the Trans-jordan plateau and below the Dead Sea, but no details are given of these successful campaigns. More is recorded about Saul's war against the Amalekites, the nomads who dwelt in the desert of the Negev and Sinai. These Bedouin tribesmen constantly raided the southern Israelite territories, killing, looting and stealing cattle and sheep. That Saul operated against them showed that his authority was accepted by the tribe of Judah, though it was only loosely associated with the Israelite tribal confederacy.

Before the expedition Samuel came to Saul and in the Lord's name declared a holy war against the Amalekites, with an injunction to spare none of them, nor their animals. Contrary to this direct order, Saul brought back as his captive the Amalekite king Agag and allowed his men to keep as booty the pick of the enemy's cattle and sheep. Once more the aged prophet flew into a terrifying rage. Saul's plea that the captured animals were intended for sacrifices was brushed aside with scorn. 'Has the Lord as great delight in burnt offerings and sacrifices, as in obeying the voice of the Lord?' (I Samuel 15:22) Saul begged for forgiveness but was spurned. Samuel demanded that Agag be produced then seized a sword and hacked him to pieces. 'Because you have rejected the word of the Lord,' Samuel shouted, 'he has also rejected you from being king.' (I Samuel 15:23) The prophet retired to his home at Ramah, and did not see the king again during his lifetime. Without Saul's knowledge Samuel sought out the young David in Bethlehem and secretly anointed him as the future king.

It is not hard to ascribe the account of this gory episode to the 'Later Source'. Samuel is the dominant figure, filled with the wrath of God. Saul is portrayed as cowed and abject before his accuser, in spite of his military prowess. To the modern mind he appears as the more humane and sympathetic character of the two. Even the statement that he had wiped out all the Amalekites except for Agag must be treated with reservation. In the next reign King David was still fighting them.

3

Saul and David

W hen Samuel rejected Saul at Gilgal at the outset of the campaign against the Philistines, he added that 'now your kingdom shall not continue; the Lord has sought out a man after his own heart; and the Lord has appointed him to be prince over his people, because you have not kept what the Lord commanded you.' (I Samuel 13:14) Again, in the second rejection scene after the Amalekite campaign, Samuel cried out to Saul: 'The Lord has torn the kingdom of Israel from you this day, and has given it to a neighbour of yours, who is better than you.' (I Samuel 15:28) (Samuel was using the symbolic fact that his robe had torn when Saul clutched it to detain him.)

These references to a successor, as yet unnamed, pave the way for David and were clearly inserted by a later editor. The same retrospective editing may account for the story of Samuel anointing the young David – a parallel to Samuel anointing Saul at Zuph.

The scene is the quiet Judean town of Bethlehem (a name meaning 'house of bread') about seven kilometres south of Jerusalem. Here Jacob was said to have buried Rachel; and in the nearby fields the charming idyll of Ruth and Boaz had taken place. David's father Jesse was a respected sheep farmer living in Bethlehem.

One day the townspeople were thrown into a flurry by an unexpected visit from that formidable man of God, Samuel. Nervously they inquired 'Do you come peaceably?' The prophet replied that he had come to offer up sacrifices to the Lord, and that they were all required to attend. Samuel especially asked to see Jesse's sons, and seven of them were presented in turn. When questioned, Jesse explained that the youngest boy was out tending the sheep; at Samuel's request he was brought in. 'Now he was ruddy, and had beautiful eyes, and was hand-some.' (I Samuel 16:12) The visiting dignitary mysteriously anointed his head with oil and then departed. The town resumed its placid life, and David went back to his sheep.

Early each morning the lad would lead his flock past the olive groves, fig trees, vegetable patches and vineyards of the valley and the terraced lower slopes and over hillsides covered with scrub and boulders to the eroded top of the ridge. From here he could gaze over the rolling expanse of the Judean hills, or down the dun-coloured wilderness to the Dead Sea and the great blue rampart of Moab beyond. In the summer heat he and the sheep would find shade behind the grey slabs of rock. During winter storms caves would shelter them from the lash of wind and rain.

David grew lithe and strong, self-confident and inured to hardship. To defend his charges against animal and bird predators, he developed a deadly aim with his sling, using smooth stones from the wadis. He produced sweet notes on a *chalil* (shepherd's pipe) and composed lyrics that he sang to the accompaniment of a *kinor* (lyre).

In his youthful fantasies David slew giants, married a king's daughter and became a great man. The urge grew within him to seek a more excit-ing future than that of a sheep farmer in a small rural town like Bethlehem.

In the outdoor solitude of the hills the young David felt God to be a close presence, an intimate father-figure who might chide him for mis-behaviour but would always protect him against his enemies. That feeling sustained him throughout his life.

King Saul began to suffer from fits of depression. In those days the explanation for mental illness was sought in theology, not medicine. The text states flatly: 'Now the Spirit of the Lord departed from Saul, and an evil spirit from the Lord tormented him.' (I Samuel 16:14) There was probably a measure of psychological truth in this diagnosis. In the earlier episodes of his reign Saul already appears to be insecure about God's approval, prone to feelings of guilt and vulnerable to Samuel's moral censure. The incident with the band of prophets, when the young Saul was carried away by their frenzied ecstasy, could be an early sign of an unstable temperament. It must have preyed on Saul's mind that Samuel, God's authorized kingmaker, had now rejected him and withdrawn from all contact with him.

The king had become a deeply disturbed man – and a dangerous one when 'the evil spirit' seized him. His worried retainers felt that music might soothe him during these attacks. Saul agreed to try. One of the servants mentioned having come across a young shepherd in Bethlehem, David the son of Jesse, who was not only skilled at making music, but also brave, clever and attractive. Saul sent for him and was so enchanted with him that he kept him at the court as the royal armour-bearer, a post of honour. When one of Saul's black moods came upon him, David played to him so sweetly on the lyre that 'Saul was refreshed, and was well, and the evil spirit departed from him.' (I Samuel 16:23)

DAVID AND GOLIATH

The Bible also relates a different way in which the young David came to the notice of King Saul. The armed struggle with the Philistines had shifted back to the disputed borderland of Samson's time – the rolling foothills of the Shefelah between the Judean range and the coastal plain. The opposing armies were encamped on opposite sides of a narrow wadi in the vale of Elah. Neither force was willing to expose itself by attacking across the open ground and up the opposite slope.

In this military stand-off the Philistines brought out their champion Goliath, a huge and powerful soldier from Gath. His height is given (with some hyperbole) as 3 metres (10 feet); his massive armour included a bronze helmet, a coat of mail weighing 68 kilograms (150 pounds), and greaves of bronze round his legs. A bronze javelin was slung across his back, a great sword in its scabbard hung from his side, and he brandished a spear with an eight-kilogram head. With his shield bearer walking before him, this human tank paraded every morning and evening between the battle lines, shouting a boastful challenge: 'I defy the ranks of Israel this day; give me a man, that we might fight together.' (I Samuel 17:10) The outcome of this single combat, Goliath added, would give the victory to one army or the other. (The practice of deciding a battle by a duel between picked champions was familiar to the Philistines, though not at that time to the Israelites.) Saul's problem was that he had no soldier willing and able to confront the gigantic Philistine on equal terms. The morale of his men was sagging badly from the daily spectacle of Goliath's contemptuous challenge.

David's three eldest brothers were serving with Saul's army. David

21

was sent by his father to bring them bread and grain from home, with ten cheeses for their commanding officer, and to return with first-hand news of their welfare. David set out at dawn down the ravine that led towards the vale of Elah, nineteen kilometres away. He arrived at the front in time to see Goliath emerge, and demanded of a group of soldiers, '. . . who is this uncircumcised Philistine that he should defy the armies of the living God'? (I Samuel 17:26) What reward, he asked them would be given to the man that killed Goliath? The answer was that he would gain wealth and would marry the king's daughter.

David's eldest brother, Eliav, showed the exasperation felt by everyone who has suffered from a cocky kid brother. He accused David of presumption, and of having come to watch the battle instead of minding his sheep. David retorted 'What have I done now? Was it not but a word?' (I Samuel 17:29) But Saul heard about this strange young man talking to his soldiers, and had him brought to the royal tent. When David offered to fight Goliath, Saul did not take him seriously. David insisted that the Lord had helped him to kill savage lions and bears that threatened his flock, and would now help him overcome the Philistine. The youth's utter faith and confidence touched the deeply religious streak in Saul. Saying 'Go, and the Lord be with you!' he put his own armour upon David and handed him his own sword. Pleading that he was unused to such encumbrances, David shed them and approached Goliath armed only with his staff, his sling and five smooth stones that he picked out of the brook.

Goliath gazed at this slight adversary with unconcealed disdain. 'Am I a dog, that you come to me with sticks . . . I will give your flesh to the birds of the air and the beasts of the field.' (I Samuel 17:43-4) David cried back that he came in the name of the Lord who did not need sword and spear. As the Philistine lumbered forward David leapt towards him, whipped out a stone and hurled it with his sling. Goliath dropped to the ground with the stone embedded in his forehead. David ran to the prostrate giant, pulled his sword out of the scabbard and lopped off his head. With this sudden and dramatic loss of their champion, the Philistines retreated, pursued by Saul's men.

Once more David was brought to Saul's tent, carrying in triumph the severed head of Goliath, and was asked to remain in the king's service. An instant friendship sprang up between him and Saul's eldest son Jonathan, who bestowed on David his own robe, armour and weapons.

SAUL'S FEUD

Handsome, skilled in battle and basking in the king's favour, the young David rose rapidly at the court and in the army, and gained the people's affection. But it is imprudent for any royal favourite to outshine his master in popularity. When they returned from military expeditions the women who welcomed them back would sing 'Saul has slain his thousands, and David his ten thousands.' (I Samuel 18:7) Saul's jealousy was aroused, and his love for David turned to a brooding and vindictive rancour. What was worse, he began to see in David (with remarkable prescience) a potential rival for the throne – '. . . and what more can he have but the kingdom? And Saul eyed David from that day on.' (I Samuel 18:8–9)

In Saul's recurrent attacks of melancholy, David would still play to him on the lyre, but the soothing effect was gone. On two occasions the frenzied king hurled his spear at his young companion, but missed him. The frightened retainers must have felt that divine providence had deflected the weapon – how else could a powerful and seasoned warrior like Saul miss his man at such a short range? A psychologist would find an answer in the love–hate conflict that divided Saul's unstable mind as he stared at the younger man.

What is more, Saul was conscious of the impact it would have on his own position if he spilt the blood of someone who had so captivated the public. But if David were to fall in battle, no blame could attach to Saul. 'Let not my hand be upon him, but let the hand of the Philistines be upon him.' (I Samuel 18:17) However, David returned unscathed from every dangerous foray, and with even greater prestige.

As an inducement to fight 'the Lord's battles' at even greater risk to his life, Saul dangled before David the prospect of marriage to his elder daughter, Merab. But the king did not seem to rate very highly the chances of David's surviving the war, because Merab in due course was married off to someone else. Saul next seized upon reports that David and the younger princess, Michal, were in love with one another.

Through the 'grapevine' of the palace staff, word reached David that the king might give his blessing to the union. David demurred, saying that his family background did not merit such an honour, and anyway he was too poor. He no doubt had in mind the *mohar*, the marriage price a groom was expected to pay the bride's father, in addition to the expensive presents bestowed on the bride. Saul was ready with an answer. The only marriage price he wanted was a hundred Philistine foreskins. The assumption was that if David attempted this 'mission impossible' he would not come back alive.

The ancient rite of circumcision had acquired a special and fundamental meaning in the Hebrew faith. Performed on male infants at the age of eight days, it marked the *brith* (covenant) between God and his chosen people. But the practice of circumcision was not confined to the Israelites; it was prevalent also among the Egyptians and the Canaanites. The Philistines were non-Semitic newcomers to the Near East, and did not share this custom, hence the Old Testament has a number of contemptuous references to them as 'the uncircumcized'. Saul's request was, therefore, not as outlandish as it may sound to the modern ear. Production of the stated number of foreskins would be the most convincing evidence that that number of Philistine soldiers had in fact been slain.

To Saul's intense chagrin David returned with his men and counted out a bagful of two hundred gory foreskins – twice the number stipulated. Saul was obliged to fulfil his side of the bargain. David was married to Michal, and became the son-in-law of the man who had been his patron and was now bent on destroying him. The family relationship did nothing to soften the king's hostility.

Caught between loyalty to his father and love for his friend David (now his brother-in-law), Jonathan tried to bring about a reconciliation. He succeeded for a while until a resurgence of Saul's homicidal compulsion put David in peril of his life. He was saved by Michal who lowered him from a window under cover of darkness and placed a dummy in his bed to deceive the men Saul had sent to watch the house. David made his way to the aged prophet Samuel at Ramah. Messengers sent there by Saul to bring David back succumbed to the religious ecstasy of the band of prophets maintained by Samuel and did not carry out their mission.

When David returned the situation remained tense. Jonathan undertook to find out what his father's attitude was, and to let David know at a secret meeting-place three days later. Meanwhile David went into hiding. When Saul demanded to know why David's place was empty at the royal table, Jonathan stated that he had gone off to visit his family in Bethlehem. Flying into one of his rages, Saul shouted abuse at Jonathan, and warned him that 'as long as the son of Jesse lives upon the earth, neither you nor your kingdom shall be established. Therefore send and fetch him to me, for he shall surely die.' (I Samuel 20:31) To underline the point Saul hurled his ever-ready javelin in Jonathan's direction. When he met his friend later, Jonathan sadly agreed that the breach was beyond repair, and that David should depart at once. They took a tearful farewell, swearing eternal friendship between them and their descendants.

Fleeing in haste, without food or a weapon, David made his way on foot to the priestly village of Nob, a few kilometres from Saul's capital of Gibeah. (It was probably located on Mount Scopus overlooking Jerusalem, near the present campus of the Hebrew University.) The chief priest of this small monastic community was Ahimelech, a direct descendant of Eli, the last high priest of the sanctuary at Shiloh. The desperate David pretended to Ahimelech that he was on an urgent and confidential mission for the king, and that his escort of young men were waiting not far away. Having no spare food, Ahimelech gave him the holy bread that had been used on the altar, as well as the only weapon on the premises – the sword David had taken from Goliath, kept as a trophy in the shrine at Nob.

The kindly priest paid a terrible price for his help. By chance the incident was observed by Doeg, the Edomite, Saul's chief herdsman, who told the king about it. In fierce anger, Saul had Ahimelech and his eighty-five fellow priests brought before him. Ahimelech protested that he had acted in innocence and good faith. How could he refuse a request from the king's son-in-law, who was 'captain over your bodyguard, and is honoured in your house'. (I Samuel 22:14) Saul brushed aside this plea and ordered his servants to slay the priests on the spot. When they shrank from this sacrilegious deed, the execution was carried out by the heartless non-Israelite, Doeg. Nob was destroyed with all the remaining inhabitants in it, and even the livestock was not spared. Only the priest Abiathar, the son of Ahimelech, escaped and eventually joined David's band of outlaws.

The fleeing David headed westward out of the Israelite hill-country and came to the Philistine city of Gath on the coastal plain, ruled over by King Achish. His hopes of remaining undetected in this enemy city were soon dashed. He was recognized as the Israelite commander whose prowess in battle had outshone that of Saul, and was hauled before Achish. The quick-witted David feigned lunacy so effectively that the Canaanite ruler impatiently asked his servants: 'Do I lack madmen, that you have brought this fellow to play the madman in my presence?'

(I Samuel 21:15) Released by his confused captors, David wasted no time in departing.

He now found refuge in a cave on Adullum, at the rocky fringe of the Hebron hills sixteen kilometres east of Gath. In this domain of boulder and bush, David attracted to himself a motley group of some four hundred followers – his brothers and kinsmen, debtors, fugitives from the law, malcontents, destitute persons and desperadoes. Fearing lest his parents might be exposed to King Saul's reprisals, he crossed the river Jordan and obtained asylum for them with the king of Moab. (According to legend, David was a descendant of Ruth the Moabite.)

What an abrupt change had occurred in David's fortunes! The shepherd boy who had risen so quickly to fame and position now found himself clinging to bare existence as leader of a brigand band.

A little to the south of Adullum was the Judean town of Keilah, in an exposed border locality. Hearing that it was being raided by the Philistines, David and his men moved in to protect it. After the rigours of their outlaw life they were doubtless glad to enjoy the amenities of a town. When Saul received a report of this move, he saw a chance of catching his elusive quarry within the confines of a walled town, and mounted an expedition to do so. With the wary instincts of a hunted man, David sensed this danger. His fellow fugitive from Saul's wrath, Abiathar, the priest from Nob, had carried away with him the *ephod*, the sacred priestly vestment that had been used in the sanctuary at Shiloh and had then been preserved at Nob. This garment was connected with divining the will of the Lord in a way that has remained a mystery. With the use of the ephod David sought God's counsel on two vital questions: Would Saul descend on Keilah? Would the townspeople then hand over David and his men? The answer in both cases was in the affirmative. Reluctantly David withdrew into the wilderness of Ziph, south-east of Hebron towards the Dead Sea.

In these southern hills, at a place called Carmel, there lived a prosperous but ill-tempered sheep farmer called Nabal. (The name means 'churlish'.) David heard that Nabal was having the feast that follows the annual shearing. He sent some of his young men to request a share of the food, pointing out that his band had protected Nabal's shepherds and flocks. The claim suggests that David kept the goodwill of the local farmers by respecting and protecting their property, and expected in exchange gifts of provisions to keep his men alive. In this case the courteous request was rejected. Nabal sneered that 'there are many servants nowadays who are breaking away from their masters.' (I Samuel 25:10) – an obvious reference to David who had fled from his master Saul. David reacted swiftly. He and his men seized their swords and set out to teach Nabal a lesson.

The frightened farm servants appealed to the farmer's comely and sensible wife Abigail. It was true, they told her, that David's men had always treated them well, and had never taken any of the animals. Now their master's rudeness was bound to provoke reprisals against them all. Without consulting her husband Abigail acted to ward off the threat. She had provisions loaded on asses and set out in the direction of David's camp. Her peace offering was impressive: '. . . two hundred loaves, and two skins of wine, and five sheep ready dressed, and five measures of parched grain, and a hundred clusters of raisins, and two hundred cakes of figs . . .' (I Samuel 25:18) When she saw David coming towards her, she alighted from her ass, bowed to the ground in front of him, and begged him to ignore her husband's rebuff. Attracted by Abigail and mollified by her plea, David took the food and turned back.

Finding her husband already drunk at the feast, Abigail did not tell him what she had done until the following morning. He flew into such a rage that he suffered a stroke and died ten days later. When David heard about this he sent messengers asking her to marry him. Without hesitating she agreed, and set out with five women servants to share with David the hard life of an outlaw.

Soon after David took another wife, Ahinoam, about whom nothing is known. Saul had meanwhile nullified his marriage to the princess Michal and had remarried her to one Palti. David had lost one wife and gained two others.

While David was hiding in the Wilderness of Ziph, Jonathan made a secret journey to seek him out. Jonathan hailed David as the future king, thereby waiving his own claim to the throne as Saul's heir. The two friends embraced and parted. They would not see one another again.

To prove their loyalty to the king and to get rid of the unwelcome outlaws in their locality, some of the men of Ziph came and told Saul where David could be found. Saul marched southward with three thousand men. He was closing in on David when word reached him that a Philistine raiding party had entered the kingdom, so he broke off the pursuit and hurried back. The respite for David was only temporary. Saul reappeared and the pressure on David and his men was resumed.

Two separate stories now follow with a common theme – David

sparing Saul's life when he was in a position to kill him. Here again, different traditions of the same event may have been preserved.

The first account is set in the bleak sandstone escarpment overlooking En-gedi, on the shore of the Dead Sea. David had been pursued to a crag with the picturesque name of Wild Goats' Rocks, and had concealed himself with some of his men at the back of a cave. As chance would have it, Saul entered the mouth of the same cave to relieve himself. David's excited followers whispered to him that this was his chance to strike back. David refused to raise his hand against 'the Lord's anointed'. Instead, he crept close to Saul in the gloom of the cave, and stealthily cut off a bit of the king's robe. David followed Saul into the open, called out to him what had happened and held up the piece of cloth as proof that he meant him no harm. Overcome with emotion Saul replied: 'You are more righteous than I; for you have repaid me good, whereas I have paid you evil.' (I Samuel 24:17) Saul then withdrew his troops.

The second incident opens with Saul and his soldiers encamped in the rough terrain of southern Judah, during his 'seek and destroy' mission against David and his band. At dead of night David and his nephew, Abishai, stole into the sleeping camp and reached the spot where Saul was lying. Again David refused to strike the defenceless king and only removed Saul's spear and the jar of water next to him. The following morning David shouted across the ravine, held up the spear and the jar and taunted Saul's general, Abner, for not keeping better guard over his master. When Saul heard the voice and came out, David demanded to know what he had done for Saul to seek his life 'like one who hunts a partridge in the mountains'. (I Samuel 26:20) The contrite Saul admitted that 'I have played the fool and have erred exceedingly' (I Samuel 26:21) and gave David his blessing before withdrawing his troops.

DAVID THE VASSAL

Life in the Judean hills had become too precarious for the outlaws, and especially for the wives and children they had acquired. David might have turned again to Samuel but the prophet had passed away and lay buried at Ramah. David took an unpalatable decision to lead his men back into Philistine territory and attach himself to Achish, King of Gath, where he would be out of Saul's reach. Achish treated his unexpected Israelite vassal well, but the proximity was no doubt uncomfortable for both. David requested that he be allowed to settle away from the royal city and he was put in charge of Ziklag, a border town between Beersheba and Gaza. From this base he led his men in forays against the Amalekites and other desert tribes that periodically raided the southern Israelites. David's tough fighting men wiped out the Amalekite encampments and seized their livestock as booty. However, in reporting to Achish, David pretended that he had carried out these expeditions against his own people, or against tribes allied to the Israelites. This devious conduct showed how sensitive his position was as a refugee wanting to keep the trust of his host, while clinging to the hope of a return to his own country. Achish at any rate, accepted what David told him, and said to himself: 'He has made himself abhorred by his people Israel; therefore he shall be my servant always.' (I Samuel 27:12)

David's relations with his masters soon became even more ambivalent, as the chronic conflict between Israel and Philistia moved towards a climax.

The coalition of the five Philistine city-states gathered their forces for a decisive battle against the Israelites, to regain the domination they had lost early in Saul's reign. The marshalling ground was at their stronghold of Aphek on the edge of the coastal plain (near modern Tel Aviv) where they had defeated the Israelites and captured the sacred Ark of the Covenant half a century earlier. From here they advanced northward into the valley of Jezreel, where they held the key fortified towns of Megiddo and Beth-shan. The control of the valley was one of vital strategic importance for two reasons. It divided the Israelite tribes in the Galilee highlands from those in the central hill-country; and through it ran the Via Maris (Way of the Sea), the main route between the Nile valley and Mesopotamia. The Philistine army pitched camp on the Moreh hill (above the present city of Jezreel) while Saul took up his position on the high ground of Mount Gilboa across the valley. With his lightly armed and nimble highlanders, Saul's battle tactics were to lure the Philistines into the hill terrain where they could not deploy their dreaded battle chariots.

David and his men brought up the rear of the Philistine advance up the coast. His predicament was resolved by the fact that the other Philistine lords distrusted these Hebrew defectors and refused to have them take part in the coming battle. What (they argued to Achish), was to prevent David from turning against them during the fighting? Achish protested that he could rely on David, but he had to yield to pressure. He apologetically told David to turn back to Ziklag with his followers.

THE DEATH OF SAUL

The day before the fateful battle Saul was in a deeply disturbed frame of mind. His experienced soldier's eye noted how formidable was the enemy force arrayed against him. Fearful of the outcome he sought divine reassurance by all the recognized channels of communication: dreams; prophets; and the casting of the sacred lots. There was no response. Feeling deserted by God, Saul tried a last desperate resort. He himself had decreed the expulsion from the kingdom of wizards, magicians and the mediums who communicated with 'familiar spirits'. These were practices banned by the Hebrew faith as being polluted with paganism. In spite of that Saul asked his servants to find out if there was in the area a medium whom he could consult. They reported that a woman who had such powers lived some miles away in the village of En-dor in the Jezreel valley near Mount Tabor. That night the disguised king went on foot to seek her out, accompanied by two faithful servants.

Knowing that such seances were illicit, the old witch was at first suspicious, fearing that her nocturnal visitor might be trying to trap her. When Saul swore to her that she would come to no harm, she complied with his strange request to summon up the spirit of Samuel. The ghost that rose up before them was as angry and unforgiving with Saul as the prophet had been while alive. He upbraided Saul for disturbing him, repeated that Saul had been rejected by the Lord, and grimly foretold that on the morrow the Israelites would be defeated, with the king and his sons slain in battle. The spirit of Samuel then vanished.

At these words of doom Saul, who had fasted all day, fell to the ground in a faint. With the help of the two retainers the woman of En-dor lifted the king on to her bed and prepared food for him. When he had recovered he returned to his own camp.

Next morning the Philistine soldiers stormed up the slopes of Gilboa and overwhelmed its defenders in fierce hand-to-hand fighting. Jonathan and his two brothers were killed. Badly wounded by the Philistine archers, the king begged his armour-bearer to kill him rather than let him fall into the hands of the enemy. The armour-bearer refused to strike at the sacrosanct person of his ruler, and Saul fell upon his own sword. The armour-bearer did likewise and died with his master.

The Philistines cut off Saul's head, hung his mutilated body on the Beth-shan city walls and exhibited his armour as a trophy, in the local temple to the goddess Astarte. When the terrible news reached the men of Jabesh-gilead (the Trans-jordan town that Saul had saved at the beginning of his reign), they recovered his body and those of his sons, buried them and fasted seven days in mourning.

The career of the first Hebrew king thus ended in a noble last stand against hopeless odds. Intent on stressing David's role, the later biblical chroniclers may have done Saul less than justice. He had been tragically unstable – moody, superstitious and liable to fits of violence. But he emerges as a brave and honourable man and a redoubtable general. He had accustomed the tribes to the overriding authority of a collective ruler, stimulated their emerging sense of nationhood, united their fighting men under a single command, and for some two decades held their external foes at bay. His reign had ended on Mount Gilboa in defeat and death; but the foundations had been laid on which David would build an empire.

4

David

Having turned back from the Philistine army at Aphek, David and his men covered the hundred and thirty kilometres to Ziklag by hard marching and arrived on the third day. A scene of desolation met their eyes. During their absence the Amalekites had seized and looted the town, set it to the torch and carried off the women and children, together with the livestock. David's exhausted and stricken men sat down and wept and then started muttering revolt against their leader, whom they blamed for leaving the town defenceless and their families exposed to Amalekite vengeance. David shook off his own grief for his two wives, and aroused his followers to set off in pursuit. At the wadi of Besor, south of Gaza, two hundred who were too tired to carry on were left behind with some of the equipment. The rest pushed forward into the open desert. Fortunately they picked up a young man who was in a state of collapse after wandering in the desert for three days. Revived by water and food, he told them that he was an Egyptian slave who had callously been abandoned by his Amalekite master when he fell sick. He guided them to the nomad encampment where the marauders were celebrating, '. . . eating and drinking and dancing, because of all the great spoil they had taken . . .'. (I Samuel 30:16) David's men launched a surprise attack at dusk. Some of the Amalekites fled on their camels; the rest were wiped out. The captive women and children were released unharmed. Their own flocks and herds were recovered, and those of the Amalekites captured. Against the protest of the men with him, David ruled that those who had been left behind at Besor should get an equal share of the spoil. (From then on it was a regular military practice that the rear echelons would be rewarded on the same basis as front line troops.) A good part of the booty was handed by David to southern Judean towns that had been friendly to him and had suffered from Amalekite raids. With his far-sighted political instincts David may have had future support in mind as well as past obligations.

The years of exile were about to end. A few days after the successful pursuit of the Amalekites, a young man arrived at Ziklag and was brought to David. His garments were torn and dust was sprinkled on his head – the traditional signs of mourning. Throwing himself on the ground before David, he blurted out that the Israelites had been routed by the Philistines on Mount Gilboa, and that Saul and Jonathan were among the slain. Questioned by David, he stated that he was the son of an Amalekite *ger* (a non-Hebrew living among the Israelites) and had happened to be on Mount Gilboa when the battle took place. He had seen the stricken king sink to the ground with the Philistines in pursuit. Saul had called him over and begged to be despatched before the Philistines caught up with him. The Amalekite claimed that he had done so, as the king was dying anyway where he lay. He had fled, carrying with him Saul's crown and armlet which he now offered to David. It is possible that the Amalekite was not telling the truth, and assumed that David would reward the man who had killed his oppressor. David ordered him put to death for having on his own admission slain the Lord's anointed. Out of David's grief came his immortal lament for Saul and Jonathan:

> Thy glory, O Israel, is slain upon thy high places!
>   How are the mighty fallen!
> Tell it not in Gath,
>   publish it not in the streets of Ashkelon;
> lest the daughters of the Philistines rejoice,
>   lest the daughters of the uncircumcised exult.
> Ye mountains of Gilboa,
>   let there be no dew or rain upon you,
>   nor upsurging of the deep!
> For there the shield of the mighty was defiled,
>   the shield of Saul, not anointed with oil . . .
> Saul and Jonathan, beloved and lovely!
>   in life and in death they were not divided;
> they were swifter than eagles,
>   they were stronger than lions . . .
> I am distressed for you, my brother Jonathan;
>   very pleasant have you been to me;
>   your love to me was wonderful, passing the love of women.
>   [II Samuel 1: 19–21, 23, 26]

After their victory the Philistines were again in virtual occupation of Israelite territory in the northern and central hill areas. Resistance was kept alive by Abner, Saul's army commander and kinsman (whether he was the king's cousin or uncle is unclear). With the remnants of his forces he retreated across the Jordan river to the Israelite district of Gilead. In its main town of Mahanaim he proclaimed Saul's surviving son as king of Israel. The youth's name had been Eshbaal (man of God) but later biblical editors contemptuously dubbed him Ishboshet (man of disgrace).

Saul's death had removed the reason for David's exile. He and his men moved into Hebron, the main city of Judah. That tribe had for a long time led an existence somewhat apart from the others, and its autonomy remained intact after the battle of Gilboa. The leading men of Judah now declared their territory an independent kingdom with David as its king and Hebron as its capital.

David sent messengers to the Trans-jordan town of Jabesh-gilead, praising its citizens for retrieving and burying the bodies of Saul and his sons. David was clearly hoping to gain the allegiance of those who had been loyal to Saul. This aim was blocked for the time being by Abner's action in declaring Saul's own son king. There were now two rival Israelite thrones and a clash between them was inevitable.

A detachment of soldiers led by Abner crossed over from Trans-jordan, presumably to assert the claims of Ishboshet. They reached Gibeon, a town in Benjamin north-west of Jerusalem. Here they were intercepted by a unit under Joab, David's nephew and army commander. The two sides started to parley, facing one another across the 'pool of Gibeon'. (Modern excavations show that this was a huge round cistern eleven metres across and ten metres deep, with a spiral staircase down the inside wall to a tunnel that led to water sources outside the city wall.) Abner proposed, and Joab agreed, that the issue be decided by individual duels between twelve picked men from each side. The men were lined up facing one another in pairs. The result seems to have been mutual elimination – 'And each caught his opponent by the head, and thrust his sword in his opponent's side; so they fell down together.' (II Samuel 2:16) With the trial of strength inconclusive general fighting broke out, with Abner's men getting the worst of it. He retreated with the survivors, pursued by Joab's men. Joab's fleet-footed younger brother, Asahel, dashed after Abner, who killed him after begging him in vain to turn aside. The consequent blood feud between Joab and Abner would cost the latter his life.

The intermittent civil war between Judah and Israel dragged on with David gradually gaining the upper hand. It was Abner who moved to resolve the conflict. A decent and upright man, he had spent many years in the field against the enemies of his people, and must have hated fighting against his fellow-Israelites. Moreover, while he had been completely loyal to the manly Saul, he now found himself serving the ineffectual youth Ishboshet for whom he felt no respect. The break came when Ishboshet accused Abner of having intercourse with Saul's concubine Rizpah. The charge had political overtones, since taking a former king's woman was a symbolic act indicating a bid for the succession. (The same tradition was to recur later in Absalom's revolt against David.) Abner secretly sent messengers to Hebron offering to help unite all the Israelite tribes under David's rule. David made only one condition – that his former wife, Saul's daughter Michal, should first be returned to him. Abner compelled Ishboshet to arrange for the delivery of his sister. Michal's devoted second husband, Palti, ran weeping behind her until ordered back by Abner. Whatever personal sentiment may have moved David, his demand was a shrewd political move, since it renewed his link with the house of Saul.

Abner prepared the ground with the notables of the northern tribes and with his own tribe of Benjamin. He then went to Hebron with an escort of twenty men to conclude the pact with David. He was warmly received and entertained for a week. Just after his departure Joab returned from an expedition and was furious to learn of these developments. Not only was Abner his blood enemy, but the accession of Saul's seasoned general to David's cause could threaten Joab's own position. His reaction was swift and ruthless. He lured Abner back on a pretext, met him at the city gate, drew him aside from his men, and stabbed him to death.

David was genuinely shocked at the murder. Moreover it set back his plans for uniting the kingdom, and left him a suspect of complicity, since it would be hard for people to believe that Joab would have acted in this way without his master's knowledge. David had Abner buried with full honours, personally eulogized him and led the mourning, starting with a day-long fast. He also publicly censured Joab and his brother and accomplice Abishai, '. . . these men the sons of Zeruiah are too hard for me. The Lord requite the evildoer according to his wickedness!'

(II Samuel 3:39) (David's sister Zeruiah was much older than he, so that her sons were his contemporaries.) Still, David refrained from punishing the 'evildoers'. Such indulgence towards his tough nephews was only human – they had been at his side through all the lean outlaw years; and he would have need of their bravery and devotion in the time to come.

Ishboshet lost heart with the removal of Abner, his kinsman and protector. Shortly after he too came to a brutal end. Two of his army officers, brothers, stole into the house while he was having a noon-day siesta, slew him on his bed and brought the severed head to David, expecting a reward. Instead they were condemned to death, just as had been the Amalekite who claimed to have killed King Saul. David gave Ishboshet's head an honourable burial in Abner's tomb at Hebron.

No obstacle remained to the unification of the northern and southern Israelite tribes under David's rule. 'So all the elders of Israel came to the king at Hebron; and king David made a covenant with them at Hebron before the Lord, and they anointed David king over Israel.' (II Samuel 5:3) He was the last Hebrew leader to be elected in the old charismatic tradition, with a mandate from the representatives of the people, in the belief that he was inspired by the Lord to save them from their foes.

One gesture by David to a member of Saul's family may be regarded as the discharge of an emotional debt, rather than an act of statecraft. At their last meeting David had promised Jonathan that if he came to power he would take care of his friend's family. Through Zeba, an old retainer of Saul's household, David learnt that Jonathan's son, Mephiboshet, was still alive. He had been five years old when his father and grandfather fell in the battle of Gilboa. In the hurried flight after that, the child was dropped, injured both legs and remained a cripple. David sent for him, had him brought up at the court with his own sons, and restored to him the lands that had belonged to Saul.

The finding of Mephiboshet probably came after a tragic episode that took the lives of all Saul's male descendants known at that time. The country had suffered a three-year drought and famine, attributed to an act of injustice committed by Saul against the Gibeonites. They formed a Canaanite enclave a few kilometres to the north-west of Jerusalem, and by a subterfuge had obtained from Joshua a treaty of guarantee. They alleged that, in his zeal to free the hill-country from non-Israelite elements, Saul had killed off some of them, thereby breaking Joshua's treaty. David offered them compensation to expiate the blood-guilt, but the Gibeonites insisted that the account could be redressed only by the blood of Saul's descendants. David had to yield and handed over to them the five sons of Saul's elder daughter Merab, and two sons Saul had had by his concubine Rizpah. The Gibeonites put all seven to death and left their bodies exposed on a rock. Rizpah spread a cloth for herself next to her slain children, and protected the bodies against crows and wild animals. Her moving vigil was maintained from the beginning of the barley harvest in early summer to the first rains in late autumn. When the drought broke, David tried to make amends by bringing the bones of Saul and Jonathan from Jabesh-gilead in Trans-jordan, and burying them, together with the bodies of the seven, in the tomb of Saul's father Kish.

THE CAPTURE OF JERUSALEM

Thirty kilometres to the north of Hebron lay Jebus (Jerusalem) the city-state of the Jebusites, a local Canaanite people. It had resisted capture during Joshua's conquest, and for the two and a half centuries since then had remained an independent enclave in the heart of Israelite territory. David boldly decided to capture it and make it the capital of his united monarchy. Jerusalem offered several advantages for this purpose. It was easily defended, being built on a narrow ridge with deep ravines on three sides. It stood at the intersection between the north–south road through the hill-country, and the east–west road from the coast across the Judean range and down to the Jordan valley. Since it was on the border between Judah and the northern tribes, and had not previously been in Israelite possession, its choice could not arouse inter-tribal jealousies.

The problem was how to conquer so formidable a stronghold. The relevant passage is one of the most cryptic in the Bible. The Jebusites declared: 'You will not come in here, but the blind and the lame will ward you off . . .'; and David said to his men: 'Whoever would smite the Jebusites, let him get up the water shaft to attack the lame and the blind. . . .' (II Samuel 5:6, 8) Apparently the defenders had lined up these afflicted persons on top of the ramparts, facing David's army – but for what purpose? The customary explanation had been that the Jebusites felt secure within their walls and were deriding their attackers. That view is unconvincing. David was renowned as a field commander; he had united the Israelite tribes behind him and was bringing their full strength to bear on overcoming an isolated Canaanite city. Its defenders could have had no cause for complacency. A more plausible interpretation is that advanced by Professor Yigael Yadin in his *The Art of Warfare in Biblical Lands*. He suggests that the Jebusites felt despondent about holding out by conventional military means and resorted to a psychological barrier based on the ancient belief in the power of a curse. The suggestion is that the Jebusites cried out to the Israelites to warn them that if they attacked, they would be cursed with the same affliction as the blind and the lame whom they could see paraded on the walls before them. It was their hope that the Israelite soldiers would hold back in fear of these bizarre defenders armed only with a supernatural belief. David offered a reward to the first man who ventured to attack, and it was the intrepid Joab who broke through.

Another textual problem concerns the 'water shaft' in the above passage. In the Hebrew text, the word is *tsinnor* which normally means a water pipe. It was rendered in the King James Bible as 'gutter'. It was supposed that the Israelites may have infiltrated through the narrow conduit that supplied the town with water from the nearby spring of Gihon. That conjecture is unsatisfactory for technical reasons. A different suggestion is that the Hebrew word means a weapon shaped like a trident. The New English Bible calls it a grappling iron, a device used for scaling defence walls. The layman can only observe with awe how the biblical scholars can dispute the meaning of a single word.

After the capture of Jerusalem David made it his capital. Nearly eight years had gone by since he had become king of Judah in Hebron. In that time the number of his wives had increased to seven, and six sons had been born to him.

During the Hebron years the Philistines had not intervened in the affairs of Judah. David may well have maintained good personal relations with his former lord, King Achish of Gath. The Philistines would anyway have been pleased to watch the internal power struggle that kept their traditional foes weak and disunited after Saul's death. But they reacted to the revival of the united monarchy under David and the spectacular capture of Jerusalem. An army was sent to wrest the city from David. It probably marched up the pass of Sorek (through which the railway now winds) and reached the open vale of Rephaim to the south-west of the walled city. David's troops repulsed them and the idols carried with their forces were captured and destroyed. When they advanced again, the Israelites fell on them from the rear at nightfall, the rustling of the balsam trees in the evening breeze being the signal to attack. The Philistines were routed and pursued back to the coastal plain.

With his hold on the city secure, David decided to bring to it the Ark of the Covenant, the most sacred cult object of the Hebrews.

The Philistines had exulted at its capture at the battle of Aphek many decades earlier, but had come to regret their troublesome prize. The Ark had been lodged at first in the temple of Dagon at Ashdod, beside the statue of the deity. The idol had toppled to the ground, and its head and arms were smashed. A plague had then struck the town; its inhabitants broke out in festering tumours and many of them died. At the same time their fields were infested with swarms of mice. Ashdod was glad to get rid of the trophy by handing it over to Gath. When that city was similarly afflicted, the Ark was bestowed on Ekron. After the same unhappy experience there the lords of the five Philistine cities consulted their priests as to whether they should send the object back to the Israelites. They assumed that the Hebrew god was deeply offended and was wreaking his vengeance on them. On the advice of the priests they put the Ark on a newly constructed cart, together with a box containing a guilt-offering of five tumours and five mice, all made of gold. Two milch cows were hitched to the cart, then turned loose to see where they would go. They headed straight for the nearest Israelite town of Beth-shemesh, thus confirming the assumption that the Israelite deity had caused the troubles during the seven months the Ark had been in their possession.

The citizens of Beth-shemesh joyfully hailed the sudden arrival of the Ark. They set up a great stone in the field where it had come to rest and sacrificed the two cows on it as a thanksgiving offering, using the cart for firewood. They were less happy when seventy of them died for having peered inside the Ark. To their relief it was taken off to the hill-top shrine of Kirjath-jearim some sixteen kilometres west of Jerusalem. Here it remained quietly for the next twenty years.

David declared a public feast day and led a great procession from Jerusalem to fetch the Ark. Again, it was placed in a new cart drawn by oxen and set out on its journey to the sound of musical instruments. Along the way a mishap occurred. The cart lurched and one of the men escorting it grabbed the Ark to steady it. He was struck dead. Fearful of the Lord's displeasure, David halted the operation and left the Ark in a nearby house, belonging to a man from Gath, presumably a man of

Philistine origin settled as a farmer in Israelite territory. When three months had passed, and it appeared that the farmer and his family were well and prosperous, David felt it was safe to move the sensitive cargo again.

In Jerusalem the Ark was installed for the time being in a huge tent, recalling the Tabernacle that had housed it when the Children of Israel had wandered in the desert under the leadership of Moses. The king led the celebrations with a symbolic dance before the Ark, clad only in a short *ephod* or priestly apron. At that moment only David was aware of the historical significance of the event. He had made Jerusalem the religious centre as well as the political capital of the Hebrew nation. At the same time he had demonstrated that the dynasty he was founding was blessed with the Lord's approval.

For David the day of happy fulfilment was marred only by an ugly quarrel with his wife Michal. Life had dealt harshly with her since the days when she had been a young and pretty princess who had fallen in love with the dashing young hero David, married him and contrived his escape from her father's jealousy. After that she had seen her father and brothers meet violent deaths and David take over the throne, while she herself was compelled to leave her second husband and share David's harem with his other wives, in order to serve his political purpose. All her bitterness and wounded pride now welled up as she watched the festivities through the window, and she lashed out at him when she went out to greet him. Was it not wonderful, she asked, to see the king leaping about and exposing his person like any worthless fellow, in front of all the common serving maids? David flung back that it was the Lord who had chosen him to reign in place of her father's house. He would go on making merry before the Lord if he thought fit, '. . . and I will be abased in your eyes; but by the maids of whom you have spoken, by them I shall be held in honour'. (II Samuel 6:22) On this unhappy note their relationship came to an end. The biblical account says laconically that she had no child to the day of her death.

DAVID'S CITY

The Jebusite city David had taken was very small. Its shape was long and narrow, stretching down along the Ophel spur to a point in the Hinnom valley, at the pool of Siloam. Its sides sloped down steeply into the Kidron valley on the east and the Tyropean valley (as it was later called) on the west. David extended the city a short distance up the ridge towards Mount Moriah, filling in a saddle for the purpose. Here he constructed a palace of stone and cedar wood, on a modest scale compared to the royal compound Solomon was to build. David had made a treaty of friendship with Hiram, king of the Phoenician port city of Tyre, who supplied him with cedar logs and skilled carpenters and masons. David also set up buildings to house the guards and the royal retinue, and a tomb for the royal family – the only persons who could be buried within the city wall. The detailed layout of David's city is still a matter of conjecture. Its remains lie under a built-up area and have not been excavated. Its northern wall was probably some two hundred metres south of the Temple Mount.

After moving to Jerusalem David acquired more wives and concubines, and numerous children were born to him. It is typical of that masculine society that only the eleven sons among them are specified by name, not the daughters.

DAVID'S EMPIRE

David followed up the victory over the Philistines in the vale of Rephaim by launching an offensive against them in the coastal plain. He occupied the city-state of Gath and subdued that of Ekron. No attempt was made to take the three Philistine cities on the coast – Ashdod, Ashkelon and Gaza – and it is assumed that they sued for terms instead of offering resistance. A shrunken Philistia remained under Israel suzerainty with its power broken. It would never again pose a serious threat to the Israelites, and in due course it became absorbed and disappeared.

The remaining Canaanite enclaves in the maritime plain and the northern valleys capitulated without a fight and were eventually assimilated into the Israelite population. Their lands became royal estates, administered by David's stewards. The Phoenician coastal strip with its two port cities of Tyre and Sidon, remained an autonomous area but within the Israelite sphere of influence. David was now the undisputed master of western Canaan.

Israelite control was pushed eastward and northward by a series of successful campaigns in Trans-jordan and Syria. Probably the toughest local war was against the Ammonite kingdom, on the plateau between the river Jordan and the desert. A new king, Hanun, had mounted the throne and David sent envoys to convey his greetings. Hanun treated them in the most insulting fashion, shaving off half their beards and slicing off the lower part of their garments from the waist. (The beard was a symbol of manhood. It was degrading to lose it and derisive to be deprived of half.) On their way back they received a message from David tactfully telling them not to come straight home, but to remain in Jericho until their beards had grown again.

The Ammonite king's conduct had invited a war. Joab was sent with an expeditionary force against the capital city, Rabbath-ammon (today's Amman). He found the Ammonite army drawn up in the open in front of the city. Hanun had previously sent to hire a mercenary army from a group of Aramean states farther to the north in southern Syria: Beth-rehob, Zobah, Maacah and Tob. The Aramean troops arrived in the rear of Joab's force, catching it in a pincer movement and forcing it to fight on two fronts. With part of his men Joab attacked the Syrians, while the rest under his brother Abishai held the Ammonites at bay. When the Syrians broke and fled, the Ammonites withdrew into their city. Since Joab did not have the strength to take it by assault, he disengaged his forces and returned to Jerusalem.

Hadad-ezer, the king of Zobah, was not prepared to accept the humiliating rout outside Rabbath-ammon. He and his allies gathered together a substantial Aramean army, that marched southward to join the Ammonites against Israel. David personally took the field at the head of his troops to counter this thrust. At the battle of Helam in northern Jordan the Arameans were defeated, their commander killed, and their chariots and horses captured. The Aramean kingdoms then accepted the status of tribute-paying vassals, and made no further attempts to intervene in the war against Ammon. An Israelite garrison was installed in the city of Damascus. The most valuable booty gained from the Syrian conquest was the copper mined in the territory of Zobah. To the north of Zobah along the Orontes river lay the important kingdom of Hamath. Its ruler sent costly gifts to David, with an offer of good-neighbour relations.

'In the spring of the year, the time when kings go forth to battle . . .' (II Samuel 11:1), Joab was sent again to lay siege to Rabbath-ammon. The resistance of the city became hopeless when Joab's soldiers gained possession of the strong points protecting the water supply. At this point Joab loyally sent a message to David, proposing that the king should come from Jerusalem and get the credit for the final capture. When the city had surrendered, David placed the crown of the deposed

Hanun upon his own head, thereby making himself king of Ammon as well. The Ammonites were used as serfs, doing menial labour.

Two further campaigns overcame the kingdoms of Moab and Edom to the east and the south of the Dead Sea. For reasons left unexplained, savage reprisals were carried out against these two peoples, and a number of them were put to death. Moab probably remained a vassal kingdom, while Edom came under direct Israel administration, with a governor appointed over it.

At that time – the beginning of the tenth century BC – Canaan was not within the orbit of any Great Power in the Near East. Through David's military and political successes, the power vacuum between the Nile and Euphrates had rapidly been filled. With its Israelite heartland, its annexed provinces and its fringe of vassal states, David's empire had emerged as the dominant force in the Canaanite–Syrian region.

The siege of Rabbath-ammon formed a backdrop to the affair between David and Bathsheba – the most romantic and the least worthy episode in David's entire career. One day towards evening David was pacing the flat roof of his palace when he looked down and saw a beautiful woman bathing herself in the courtyard of a nearby house. Overcome with desire for her, David sent to find out who she was. Her name was Bathsheba and she was married to a foreign officer in his army, Uriah the Hittite, who was serving with Joab against the Ammonites. David had her brought to the palace and made love to her. Some while after he received from her the simple but alarming message: 'I am with child.'

The obvious way to avoid a high-level scandal was for Uriah to have access to his wife as soon as possible. David sent a dispatch to Joab requesting that Uriah return to Jerusalem, ostensibly to report to the king on the course of the war. When he arrived David asked him some questions and released him to go to his home. To the king's chagrin Uriah stayed the night at the palace with his fellow officers. When David urged him next day to relax at home after the journey, Uriah solemnly replied that 'my lord Joab and the servants of my lord are camping in the open field; shall I then go to my house, to eat and to drink, and to lie with my wife?' (II Samuel 11:11) Even plying him with drink did not break down Uriah's tiresome self-denial. When he went back to the front after two days in Jerusalem, David gave him a sealed letter for Joab. It was very explicit: 'Set Uriah in the forefront of the hardest fighting . . . that he may be struck down, and die.' (II Samuel 11:15) Joab included him in an attack on a well-defended sector of the city wall, where he was one of the casualties from the enemy archers. After Bathsheba had observed the prescribed period of mourning, David married her. In due course she gave birth to an infant son.

Nathan, the court prophet, normally a somewhat colourless person, found the courage to raise his voice on behalf of his master, the Lord. He appeared before David and with great pathos related a parable. It concerned a rich man with many flocks and herds, and a poor man who owned nothing but one ewe lamb that was reared in the bosom of his family. When an important visitor needed to be entertained, the rich man took away the ewe lamb to prepare the meal.

David exclaimed indignantly that a man who could do that deserved to die. Dramatically Nathan pointed to the king and cried out 'you are the man'. David, he said, had sinned in the eyes of the Lord, and evil would rise up against him out of his own household. As for the child born to Bathsheba, its life would be forfeited. The infant fell ill; in the hope of saving it David fasted, prayed, wept and lay prostrate on the ground. When it died a week later, David astonished his retainers by getting up, dressing and eating as usual. He explained sadly to them: 'Can I bring him back again? I shall go to him, but he will not return to me.' (II Samuel 12:23) Bathsheba conceived again, and bore David another son, who was called Solomon.

THE ORGANIZATION OF THE KINGDOM

It was politic for David to preserve a sense of continuity with the past. Nominally the tribal system remained intact. The Ark of the Covenant rested once more in a central sanctuary, as it had done at Shiloh in the period of the Judges. But the old order had started breaking down in the reign of Saul; and under David, central government developed rapidly. The authority of the king became paramount, superseding that of the local tribal elders. 'So David reigned over all Israel, and David administered justice and equity to all his people.' (II Samuel 8:15) Jerusalem administered a domain that extended far beyond the original Israelite territory and included a number of non-Israelite peoples.

Grouped round David at the court was a cabinet of 'king's men', who held office by his favour alone, and not as tribal leaders. The most influential among them was Joab, in charge of the armed forces. Jehoshaphat the *mazkir* (recorder) looked after the court records and served as official chronicler. Seruiah, the *sofer* (scribe), was the chief executive officer responsible for drafting and carrying out the royal decrees. Benaiah commanded the foreign mercenaries, including the Philistine bodyguard. Adoniram served David and later Solomon in the unpopular task of levying the corvée or forced labour for building and construction. By the time of the Absalom revolt the chief royal counsellor was the subtle Ahithophel.

Both secular and religious power were concentrated in David's hands, and the heads of the spiritual establishment were subordinate to him. The two high priests he appointed were Abiathar, who had been with him from the early days, and Zadok, whose origin is unknown. (One theory is that he had been the local Jebusite priest, and was taken over by David.) Nathan and Gad were the resident prophets at the court.

Apart from the names and tasks of these men, few details are given about the way David's kingdom was organized and administered. The main sources of royal revenue were the tribute payments from vassals and the income from the extensive royal estates and properties.

In the period of the Judges the Israelites had no professional warrior caste. In an emergency each tribe called up its able-bodied men, who went back to their normal pursuits when the danger was over. The kingship of Saul saw the beginning of a small cadre of full-time soldiers. David's continuous campaigns, and the control of the empire he carved out, produced a much more extensive and elaborate system of military organization.

The brunt of the campaigns was carried by a regular army, with Joab as its commander-in-chief and his brother Abishai as his deputy. This army was composed partly of Israelite units and partly of foreign mercenaries, mainly elements of the Philistine population – Cherethites (Cretans), Perethites (Philistines) and Gittites (men of Gath).

The Bible cites by name a number of warriors in David's army as battle heroes or 'mighty men'. First came a special group of three whose deeds sound like a citation for the Victoria Cross in the British army or the Congressional Medal of Honour in the American forces. The rest of them formed an elite group called 'the thirty' (actually thirty-three are mentioned). Their leader was Abishai and the group also included Benaiah. Other names included in the list are: Asahel, Joab's youngest brother who was killed by Abner after the battle of Gibeon; Uriah, the Hittite, the unfortunate husband of Bathsheba; and Eliam, the son of David's counsellor Ahithophel and perhaps the father of Bathsheba. It is a matter of conjecture whether 'the thirty' carried out a collective function as an army council or general staff. Most of them were veterans from David's fugitive days at Adullam.

At some stage during David's reign the tribal levies were also organized into a part-time militia. Twelve formations were set up, each consisting of twenty-four thousand men and commanded by one of the senior career officers. In rotation, one of these formations was on duty for each month of the year. When the need arose, several or all of them could be called up. The men for this militia were supplied by the tribal authorities. The modern army of the State of Israel follows this basic division between full-time units and reserve units doing an annual period of training.

The controversial census ordered by David late in his reign was probably meant to collect the data required for the militia arrangements, though some scholars suggest that it formed a basis for taxation. That its primary purpose was military is shown by putting Joab (much against his will) in charge of the census, assisted by a team of army officers. Moreover the people to be listed were defined as the 'valiant men that drew the sword'. Joab's group started at Aroer, east of the Dead Sea, worked its way up Trans-jordan to the vicinity of Dan in the extreme north-east, crossed over to the coast near Tyre, came down through Beersheba and then returned to Jerusalem, nine months and twenty days after they had set out. The tally is given as five hundred thousand for Judah and eight hundred thousand for 'Israel' – that is, the rest of the country.

The census flouted an ancient taboo against counting people or even livestock and possessions. An epidemic broke out which religious spokesmen attributed to God's anger. The prophet Gad advised David to make amends by building an altar and offering a sacrifice on the threshing floor of Araunah the Jebusite, on top of Mount Moriah. David bought the site from Araunah for fifty shekels (six hundred grams) of silver. The oxen used for the threshing were included in the deal, and were sacrificed. The pestilence came to an end. The threshing floor was to become the site of Solomon's Temple.

It seems strange that David did not himself build the Temple as a permanent abode for the Ark he had brought to Jerusalem. That he had in mind to do so was revealed in his remark to the prophet Nathan: 'See now, I dwell in a house of cedar, but the Ark of God dwells in a tent.' (II Samuel 7:2) The matter came up at a time when 'the Lord had given him rest from all his enemies round about' (II Samuel 7:1) – that is, when David's empire had been established and he could give his attention to a Temple project.

At first Nathan encouraged David; but the following morning he came back with an adverse reaction from the Lord. What need did God have for a house, said Nathan, when he had been 'moving about in a tent for my dwelling' since the Exodus from Egypt? In this reply one can detect a note of longing for the freedom and simplicity of the nomad past in the desert, as compared with life in built-up cities. The passage is built round a pun: instead of David giving the Lord a 'house' (i.e. a temple), the Lord promised David a 'house' (i.e. a dynasty).

The Book of Chronicles (much later in date than the Book of Samuel) offers a rational explanation. In his farewell address to a great assembly he had convened, David declared 'I had it in my heart to build a house of rest for the ark of the covenant of the Lord . . . but God said to me "You may not build a house for my name, for you are a warrior and have shed blood".' (I Chronicles 28:2–3) According to the chronicler, David handed over to Solomon the detailed plan for the Temple, and the gold, silver, gems and materials he had accumulated for the project. David is thus in retrospect given a major share of the credit for Solomon's Temple.

THE REVOLT OF ABSALOM

Amnon was David's eldest son, his mother being Ahinoam. The second son, Chileab, is not mentioned again after his birth to Abigail, and probably died young. Maacah the mother of his third son Absalom was the daughter of Talmai, king of Geshur, a tiny Aramean vassal-state on the Golan Heights east of the Sea of Galilee. Absalom was a young man of striking beauty, with very thick and lustrous hair. (It is recorded with pride that the amount cropped at his annual haircut weighed two hundred shekels – about 2.5 kilograms or 5 pounds.)

Amnon became tormented by desire for Absalom's beautiful young sister (and his own half-sister) Tamar. He was at a loss how to make advances to her, especially as she was still a virgin. On the advice of a sly cousin he pretended to be ill. When his father came to see him Amnon begged that Tamar should come to his quarters and bake him some of his favourite cakes. David arranged that this should be done. When alone in the room with the girl Amnon proposed that she should come to bed with him. She protested that this would be wrong, and asked why he did not ask their father for her hand (a marriage between a half-brother and half-sister was still permitted at that time, though later forbidden). Overcome with lust Amnon raped her. As so often happens, his guilt feelings turned against the victim, and he had her thrown out of his house by a servant. Wailing with shame Tamar tore her gown, put ashes on her head and ran to take refuge with Absalom, in whose home the 'desolate woman' remained.

The rape of Tamar was to have consequences that shook the kingdom, and eventually opened the way for the succession of Solomon, far down the seniority list of David's sons. But at first the incident seemed to be forgotten except by the dishonoured girl. David was angry with Amnon but took no action – being more ineffectual and indulgent as a parent than he was in other matters. What was more surprising, the proud and impetuous Absalom seemed to take the affair calmly. He was biding his time; and two years later he took his revenge.

All the princes, including Amnon, were prevailed upon to attend the annual shearing festival at Absalom's sheep farm in the hills of Ephraim. After Amnon had been plied with wine, Absalom ordered his servants to kill him. The others mounted their mules and rushed back to Jerusalem in panic. Absalom himself fled to his maternal grandfather, the king of Geshur.

In time David became reconciled to the murder of Amnon and longed to see the attractive Absalom, who had been his favourite son. Sensing this, Joab contrived an ingenious way of influencing the king. A woman from the village of Tekoa, ten kilometres south of Bethlehem, obtained an audience with David. She told him she was a widow, one of whose sons had killed the other in a quarrel. Her kinsmen demanded that the culprit be surrendered and put to death. She pleaded that if this punishment were carried out, no one would be left to look after her or preserve her late husband's name. David ruled that the remaining son should be left alive and promised to protect her against her angry family. She then cautiously suggested that in the same way the king should pardon his own erring son, Absalom. David at once suspected that Joab was behind the interview, which she admitted when he taxed her with it. But the stratagem had achieved its purpose. Joab was sent to Geshur to fetch Absalom back after a three-year exile. Yet to his dismay, his father had not forgiven him and refused to receive him. Two years went by, with Absalom growing more bitter at his rejection. His cousin, Joab, also refused to see the young man; after two vain attempts to reach him Absalom forced a meeting by setting Joab's barley field on fire. When Joab's anger blew over, he agreed to intercede once more with the king. A tearful reunion then took place between father and son.

However Absalom's resentment of his father had by now gone beyond any hope of a genuine reconciliation. He started undermining the king's standing with the public and building up a following of his own. Absalom would go through Jerusalem in a chariot with an escort of fifty men clearing the way, as if he were already the monarch. Early each morning he would station himself at the city gate, intercept men coming from the various tribes to seek the king's justice, and tell them they would fail to get a hearing until he, Absalom, was the judge in the land. After four years of fanning grievances and building up contacts, Absalom raised the standard of revolt. He proclaimed himself king in Hebron and sent messengers through the country to rally tribal leaders to his cause.

In the normal course Absalom, as the eldest surviving son, would have been regarded as the natural heir to the throne. But there was no law or fixed tradition to that effect. David had the right to decide the succession, and Absalom was convinced that it would be decided against him – hence the bid to seize power by force.

It looked at first as if the gamble would succeed. The years of systematic subversion bore fruit. The handsome and popular prince was suddenly the catalyst for all the multiple discontents in the realm. Hebron felt it had been pushed aside by the removal of the capital to Jerusalem. The autonomy of the individual tribes had too rapidly been displaced by the monarchic power at the centre. The northern tribes, grouped together as 'Israel', were not reconciled to domination by Judah. The non-Israelite peoples conquered by David hoped for liberation. About the court there were, as in all courts, individuals who felt disgruntled for one reason or another. 'And the conspiracy grew strong, and the people with Absalom kept increasing.' (II Samuel 15:12) The most important single recruit was David's sagacious counsellor Ahithophel, who accepted an invitation to join the rebel prince in Hebron.

David was caught completely by surprise. He had not taken seriously enough the trouble-making by his wayward son, and had underrated the signs of disaffection in his kingdom. Kings are not as a rule told unpleasant truths by their courtiers! When the full danger burst upon him, his instinctive reaction was to get away with followers he could trust, instead of being trapped in the city. He decided to head eastward across the Jordan river, beyond which there were reliable garrisons and loyal vassals.

In the Kidron valley below the eastern wall, David stood at the side of the road to see who had followed him. When Ittai from Gath marched up at the head of a regiment of his countrymen, David urged them to go back, pointing out that as Philistine mercenaries they had no duty to set off wandering with him. Ittai refused to leave his master.

The two high priests, Abiathar and Zadok, came up with a retinue of Levites, carrying with them the most precious of all Hebrew treasures, the Ark of the Covenant. Beneath the stress of the moment, David's cool and resourceful mind was already planning ahead. The high priests were told to go back and resume their functions. They were to serve as David's eyes and ears in the capital. He would wait at the Jordan river ford for a report from them, and their respective sons, Ahimaaz and Jonathan, would be used as runners.

Crossing the Kidron valley, David went up the Mount of Olives '. . . weeping as he went, barefoot and with his head covered'. (II Samuel 15:30) All who followed him were in tears. At the top of the hill he was met by his close friend and adviser Hushai the Archite, one of a Canaanite clan north of Jerusalem that had been assimilated. David saw a chance to augment the fifth column left behind in Jerusalem. Hushai was instructed to attach himself to Absalom and to counteract the influence of Ahithophel, who was now master-minding the takeover. Reports from Hushai could be relayed to David through the high priests.

On the way down to the Jordan valley there were two disturbing encounters. Zeba, the old retainer from Saul's household now serving Jonathan's crippled son Mephibosheth, brought David a gift of two riding asses, loaded with bread, fruit and wine. When David asked about the boy he had adopted, the servant answered that his young master had remained behind in the hope of gaining the throne as heir to Saul. Deeply hurt, David promised all Mephibosheth's property to Zeba.

As they neared the river, there suddenly appeared on the slope above them an old Benjamite called Shimei, a distant kinsman of Saul. Dancing with malignant glee, he flung stones at the weary men below and shrilly reviled David: 'Begone, begone, you man of blood, you worthless fellow! The Lord has avenged upon you all the blood of the house of Saul, in whose place you have reigned; and the Lord has given the kingdom into the hand of your son Absalom. See, your ruin is upon you; for you are a man of blood.' (II Samuel 16:7–8) David restrained Abishai from rushing at the old man and killing him on the spot. He remarked sadly: 'Behold, my own son seeks my life; how much more now may this Benjaminite! Let him alone, and let him curse; for the Lord has bidden him.' (II Samuel 16:11) It was not the moment to open another blood feud with the house of Saul, and to give another grievance to Saul's tribe of Benjamin. The account with Shimei was left unsettled for the time being.

Absalom entered Jerusalem in triumph. To his great surprise, he was greeted at the gate by Hushai. Ironically Absalom was horrified to see that David's close companion had deserted him. 'Is this your loyalty to your friend? Why did you not go with your friend?' (II Samuel 16:17) Hushai humbly explained that just as he had served David he would now serve the son whom the Lord and the people had chosen as king. The flattered Absalom took him at his word.

Acting on the advice of Ahithophel, Absalom demonstrated the change of regime in the most carnal and conspicuous fashion. He pitched a tent on the flat roof of the palace and had intercourse with each of the ten concubines David had left behind in his harem. These women were royal possessions and the public had no difficulty in understanding that the action symbolized Absalom's succession.

Having worked closely with him, Ahithophel knew that even on the run David remained a formidable and dangerous foe. If the revolt was to succeed it was essential to eliminate David at once, before he could recover and rally support. Ahithophel came to Absalom and offered to set out that same night in pursuit of David with twelve thousand men, in order to attack and kill him while he was still weary and discouraged. 'I will strike down the king only, and I will bring all the people back to you as a bride comes home to her husband.' (II Samuel 17:2, 3) Absalom was agreeable, but before finally deciding wanted to hear Hushai's opinion as well. Hushai understood as clearly as Ahithophel that David desperately needed to gain time, and shaped his advice accordingly. Ahithophel's plan, he argued, could easily go wrong. It did not sufficiently take into account that '. . . your father and his men are mighty men, and that they are enraged, like a bear robbed of her cubs in the field'. (II Samuel 17:8) The attackers would suffer heavy casualties and their morale would break. Besides, a wily old fighter like David would not be caught in the camp, but would have hidden himself somewhere apart. Would it not be more prudent, asked Hushai, to raise a large army by calling up the tribal levies? They could then make certain that David and his men could be overwhelmed. Hushai was shrewdly playing on the fear of David's military prowess, and that of the grizzled veterans with him.

Absalom and his leading supporters were impressed by Hushai's counsel of caution, and started debating the merits of the two conflicting courses of action presented to them. Hushai wasted no time in getting a message to David through the high priests and their sons, urging him to cross into Trans-jordan in case Absalom should approve Ahithophel's plan. The two runners were spotted and chased by Absalom's soldiers but got away with the help of a kindly housewife in the village of Bahurim, east of Jerusalem, who hid them in her well until the coast was clear. They reached David that night. Before dawn the whole of his party had forded the river.

Absalom and his advisers concluded that 'the counsel of Hushai the Archite is better than the counsel of Ahithophel'. (II Samuel 17:14) Ahithophel's lucid intellect at once grasped the implications. His opinions had been received until then '. . . as if one consulted the oracle of God'. (II Samuel 16:23) This time he had gambled and failed. He foresaw that the insurrection was doomed to an inevitable and tragic end, and refused to wait passively for his own fate. Saddling his ass, he quietly went off to his native town of Giloh. There he set his affairs in order and hanged himself.

David put to good use the time Hushai had gained for them. He made his base at Mahanaim in Gilead, located in the canyon of the Jabbok tributary that joined the river Jordan near the Adam ford. (It was here in Mahanaim that Abner had proclaimed Ishbosheth king after the death of Saul.) The land of Gilead, the Israelite territory east of the Jordan opposite the hills of Ephraim, was a good choice of ground for the looming battle. David's experienced commanders and regular soldiers were better able to exploit the rough and thickly wooded terrain than were Absalom's ill-trained and hastily assembled militia. The local population in Gilead had remained loyal to David. When he and his people arrived without provisions or field equipment, such basic needs as sleeping mats, bowls, jugs and supplies of grain, sheep, cheese and honey were brought by three prominent supporters – Shobi, Machir and Barzillai. Shobi was the brother of the Ammonite king Hanun against whom David had fought, and he had probably been installed by David as governor in Rabbath-ammon after its capture.

David organized his troops into three formations, commanded respectively by Joab, Abishai and Ittai the Gittite. They insisted that the king should remain in overall charge at Mahanaim instead of leading the army in person. Their reasoning was straightforward: if they were defeated, Absalom's forces would not bother to press the pursuit if David was not with them. David agreed but made one stipulation: 'Deal gently for my sake with the young man Absalom.' (II Samuel 18:5)

Absalom's army crossed the river under the command of his cousin Amasa, another nephew of David by his sister Abigail. The battle took place in 'the forest of Ephraim', so called perhaps, because the district had been settled by men of that tribe. Absalom's troops were routed and they fled. In trying to escape on his mule through the trees, Absalom's head was caught and wedged between the overhanging branches of an oak tree. He was jerked out of the saddle and left dangling helplessly. One of Joab's men came upon him and rushed back to tell his commander. Joab ignored David's order to spare Absalom's life. He drove three darts into Absalom's chest, then ordered his armour bearers to cut the young man down and finish him off. The body was flung into a pit and covered with a heap of stones. Joab gave a blast on his trumpet as a signal for his men to disengage and return to base.

Joab had to send off a runner to inform David in Mahanaim about the successful outcome of the battle. Ahimaaz, the son of the high priest Abiathar, volunteered to go. However Joab did not think it suitable that Ahimaaz should also have to bring the report about Absalom: '. . . you may carry tidings another day, but today you shall carry no tidings, because the king's son is dead'. (II Samuel 18:20) Instead Joab sent an Ethiopian slave. Ahimaaz went on insisting and in the end Joab permitted him to go as well. Ahimaaz did not follow the Ethiopian by the direct route across the hills; he took a longer but easier way through the Jordan valley, and arrived first at Mahanaim. He reported on the victory, but when David asked about Absalom, Ahimaaz did not have the courage to break the news, and mumbled an evasive reply. A little later the Ethiopian runner was brought in, and came out with the truth.

David was so overcome with grief that the victory was for the moment pushed out of his mind. He went up to the roof-chamber over the gate and wept, crying out as he went: 'O my son Absalom, my son, my son Absalom; Would I had died instead of you, O Absalom, my son, my son!' (II Samuel 18:33)

The unrepentant Joab came back and found the king withdrawn into his room, an air of mourning in the town, and the soldiers slinking back as if they had been defeated. Joab burst into David's chamber and gave him a blunt scolding: '. . . you love those who hate you and hate those who love you. For you have made it clear today that commanders and servants are nothing to you . . . if Absalom were alive and all of us were dead today, then you would be pleased.' (II Samuel 19:6) He roughly demanded that David show himself to his soldiers and praise them for saving the day. David was jolted into an awareness of his duties as king. He pulled himself together, and went out to review his men.

The upheaval caused by the rebellion had left the kingdom in a confused and disorganized state. David received word that the northern tribes (Israel) were talking of appealing to him to resume his rule after the collapse of the revolt. However it was more important to David that he should first regain the allegiance of his own tribe of Judah. It had always been his political power-base; moreover, it was in Judah that Absalom's revolt had started. Through the two high priests in Jerusalem, David obtained an invitation from the notables of Judah to return, and the men of Judah went down in a body to Gilgal in the Jordan valley in order to escort him back across the river ford.

There were others who were received by David at the river. Shimei the Benjaminite sought pardon for having heaped imprecations on the king on the memorable day when David had fled. Overriding Abishai's anger, David spared the old man's life. The time, he reckoned, called for clemency, not revenge.

Mephibosheth, Jonathan's lame son, came to explain that he had wanted to ride out with David at the time of the revolt, but had been deceived into staying behind by the retainer Ziba. Unwilling to spend time investigating where the truth lay, David ruled that Mephibosheth and Ziba should each keep half the property left behind by Saul.

The eighty-year-old Barzillai the Gileadite, among the first to supply David with provisions and necessities when he had reached Mahanaim, had accompanied the king to Gilgal. Invited by David to reside in the palace in Jerusalem, Barzillai pleaded that he wished only to return to his own town and be buried in the family tomb. Instead his son Chimham remained with David.

The priority David had given to restoring his relations with his own tribe brought to the surface the latent antagonism between Judah and Israel. The northern tribes had not been informed in advance of his return, and had been left out of the official welcome by the leaders of Judah. Gilgal was in the territory of Benjamin, which David had to cross on his way to Jerusalem. A large crowd of Benjaminites had come down to the river with Shimei, and men from other northern tribes had probably joined them. After David had crossed the river, they complained to him that the notables of Judah had 'stolen you away'. A bitter quarrel broke out between the two groups. The Judah delegation claimed the prerogative because David was of their tribe. The spokesmen of Israel maintained that they had no lesser share in the king, and had been the first to speak of bringing him back. In the heat of the controversy one of the Benjaminites, Sheba the son of Bichri, blew a trumpet and shouted out: 'We have no portion in David, and we have no inheritance in the son of Jesse; every man to his tents, O Israel!' (II Samuel 20:1) He led away the men of Israel in protest, and only the men of Judah accompanied David up to Jerusalem.

As a gesture of conciliation to the elements in Judah that had supported Absalom, David had appointed Amasa, his nephew and Absalom's general, as commander-in-chief of the army instead of Joab, whom he had not forgiven for the killing of Absalom. Amasa's first task was to suppress the Sheba revolt before it could gain momentum. David instructed him to organize an expeditionary force and report back in three days. When he failed to do so David dispatched Abishai with the palace guards to deal with the trouble. Amasa met them along the road near Gibeon, and was murdered by the deposed Joab, who had accompanied his brother Abishai. Sheba and his followers were pursued northward and took refuge in the walled town of Abel-beth-maacah in the north-east corner of the country, near Dan. Joab, who had now taken charge, laid siege to the place and prepared to storm it. A 'wise woman' of the town came close to the parapet and negotiated a deal with Joab: she would get the citizens to kill Sheba and throw his severed head over the wall. When this was done, Joab abandoned the siege and marched back to Jerusalem. David reluctantly reinstated him in his previous post.

David had taken the Sheba revolt very seriously, even stating that '... Sheba the son of Bichri will do us more harm than Absalom'. (II Samuel 20:6) As it turned out this seemed an unduly alarmist view; the uprising was ended quickly and with hardly any bloodshed. In the long run, David's assessment was prophetic. The episode had been an ominous reminder that the merger of north and south, of Israel and Judah, was more brittle than it appeared. The united monarchy would be held together by the two most remarkable rulers in Jewish history, David and his son Solomon. On the latter's death, it would split wide open.

In David's declining years, the reins of government started slipping from his hands, and he gave himself over more and more to meditation. Throughout his long and turbulent career he had lived in intimate communion with God and under his protection. In a hymn of praise his faith as a Hebrew and his pride as a king blended with the pastoral scenes of his boyhood.

> The spirit of the Lord speaks by me,
>   his word is upon my tongue.
> The God of Israel has spoken,
>   the Rock of Israel has said to me:
> When one rules justly over men,
>   ruling in the fear of God,
> he dawns on them like the morning light,
>   like the sun shining forth upon a cloudless morning,
> like rain that makes grass to sprout from the earth. [II Samuel 23: 2–4]

As his bodily vigour waned, he trembled with cold however many clothes he wore. His worried retainers brought him a beautiful young girl, Abishag the Shunammite from the valley of Jezreel, and said to him, '. . . let her wait upon the king, and be his nurse; let her lie in your bosom, that my lord the king may be warm'. (I Kings 1:2) She took tender care of him, and her youth and looks gave him solace, though he 'knew her not'.

The troublesome question of the succession had not been finally settled in the years since Absalom's death. It became acute now that David was nearing his end. The most likely heir was the eldest surviving son, the handsome Adonijah. He decided to assert his claim instead of waiting for David to make a formal choice. In this, he was supported by two powerful men close to the king, Joab the commander-in-chief and Abiathar the high priest. Adonijah invited a gathering of sympathetic notables to the spring of En-rogel in the Kidron valley south-east of the city. Here he sacrificed sheep and oxen on a sacred rock known as the

Serpent's Stone, after which they all sat down to a feast in his honour, already addressing him as king.

Adonijah rightly surmised from which circle his claim might be challenged. He had invited all the younger royal princes except Solomon; and he had also omitted Nathan the prophet, Zadok the other high priest, and Benaiah the commander of the palace guard – all of whom, he suspected, would try to form a rival faction.

On Nathan's advice Bathsheba came into David's chamber, told him what Adonijah had done and reminded him of his promise that her son Solomon would succeed him. As arranged with Bathsheba, Nathan then came in and backed her plea. David sent for Zadok and Benaiah, and ordered that Solomon be taken on the royal mule to the spring of Gihon, anointed as king and seated on the throne. Zadok performed the anointing ceremony with sacred oil from the Tabernacle of the Ark. The trumpet was blown and the crowd that had gathered shouted 'Long live King Solomon!'

When the group feasting with Adonijah heard the noise and learnt what had caused it, they promptly dispersed. Fearing for his life Adonijah rushed to the altar and grasped its protruding horns, the customary way of gaining sanctuary. The youthful Solomon, already acting with regal authority, assured Adonijah that he had nothing to fear as long as he remained in his house and caused no trouble.

On his deathbed David enjoined Solomon to 'be strong, and show yourself a man, and keep the charge of the Lord your God, walking in his ways . . .' (I Kings 2:2, 3) He then instructed Solomon to settle accounts with Joab for the murders of Abner and Amasa, and with Shimei the Benjaminite who had cursed David when he fled Jerusalem. Solomon was to be kind to the sons of Barzillai, the Gileadite who had helped David at the time of Absalom's revolt. 'Then David slept with his fathers, and was buried in the city of David.' (I Kings 2:10) He had reigned for forty years (1000–961 BC), seven in Hebron and thirty-three in Jerusalem.

THE DAVID DOCUMENT

It is generally accepted by scholars that the story of David's reign from his first sight of the lovely Bathsheba (II Samuel 11:2) to the succession of Solomon and the death of David (I Kings 2) are the work of a single unknown author who had first-hand knowledge of the events described.

The central theme is the struggle over the succession, involving David's sons Amnon, Absalom, Adonijah and Solomon. The account was probably drawn up during Solomon's reign and at his instigation. One theory is that the writer was Ahimaaz, the son of Abiathar the high priest.

These eighteen chapters are the finest narrative writing in the entire Old Testament. They have a dramatic flow of action, vivid personal details, and a superb and concise style. Above all the document is remarkable because it refuses to be a conventional eulogy of a departed monarch. The figure of David emerges in the round, with all its complexity and contradiction. He is a man of dazzling gifts, a warrior, statesman and empire builder, yet also a dreamer and poet. He is God-fearing and humble in his faith, yet capable of being an opportunist and a sinner. With all his shrewd political judgement and his understanding of men and power, he could be obtuse and even weak with his own children. The greatest ruler the Hebrew race produced, David is also the most fascinating human personality in the Old Testament.

By popular belief, the Book of Psalms in the Old Testament was the work of the great king who became known as 'the sweet psalmist of Israel'. (II Samuel 23:1) Of the hundred and fifty psalms in the Book, seventy-three actually contain the phrases 'of David' in their titles, and many of these are written in the first person. The beauty and fervour of this exalted religious poetry have stirred Jews and Christians alike down the ages, and are part of the legacy of all mankind. Their actual origin and age are obscure and have long been debated by scholars.

The Book (also known as the psalter) was clearly compiled from several collections produced in different periods. According to their themes, the psalms can be grouped into hymns in praise of God; laments for personal suffering or national disaster; songs of thanksgiving; 'Zion songs' extolling Jerusalem, the holy city; 'royal psalms' referring to the anointed king; and didactic poems stressing wisdom and good conduct. The generic title in Hebrew, *Tehillim* (praises), came into use in the early Talmudic period. One of the Dead Sea Scrolls contains thirty-four psalms found in the present Book, as well as seven not previously known.

Recent research suggests that a number of the psalms actually date from David's time and therefore could have been written or inspired by him. The traditional association of his name with this Book is a natural one, for much of its contents sound like an expression of his experiences and emotions.

5

Solomon

It is unlikely that David would have passed over older sons and handed his throne to an inexperienced youth, unless he had recognized special qualities in him.

Solomon did indeed have the capacity to consolidate and organize the kingdom carved out by his father. In place of the conflict and drama of David's reign, the nation had relative peace and prosperity for the thirty-nine years that Solomon occupied the throne (961–922 BC).

After David's death the new king showed he could act decisively against the men who had opposed him or injured his father, and who might still have been a threat to him in the future.

The first in that accounting was Adonijah, David's eldest surviving son, who had made an abortive bid to seize the throne. He was foolish enough to ask for Abishag, who had looked after David before he died. Since this could be interpreted as a symbolic claim to the succession, Solomon promptly took the opportunity to order his elder brother's execution.

Abiathar the high priest had backed Adonijah, but his life was spared because of the many years of faithful service he had given David. He was dismissed from his office and banished from the capital to his home in the hamlet of Anathoth outside Jerusalem.

Joab, realizing that he was in mortal danger, took sanctuary at the altar. At Solomon's express command, the tough Benaiah, commander of the palace guard, cut Joab down while he was still grasping the altar horns. Solomon justified this unprecedented act by the need to wipe out the blood-guilt for the murders he had committed. Benaiah was rewarded with Joab's post as commander-in-chief of the army.

There remained Shimei, the old Benjaminite who had placed a curse on David when he fled from Absalom. Solomon ordered him not to leave Jerusalem on penalty of death. One day Shimei went to Gath looking for two runaway slaves. On his return Solomon had him put to death by Benaiah. 'So the kingdom was established in the hand of Solomon.' (I Kings 2:46)

The young king went to the shrine at Gibeon to make sacrifices. There the Lord appeared to him in a dream and asked him what he desired. Solomon answered: 'Give thy servant . . . an understanding mind to govern thy people, that I may discern between good and evil.' (I Kings 3:9)

The first time Solomon's sagacity was put to the test produced one of the most celebrated judgements in history. Two harlots living in the same house gave birth to infants, one of whom died. Each claimed that she was the mother of the surviving child. When they appeared before the king, he ruled that the child should be cut in two and one half given to each of the women. One of them accepted the verdict. The second cried out that she would renounce her claim for the sake of the child. Solomon awarded her the baby as she was obviously its real mother.

Solomon inherited the throne when the era of military campaign and conquest under Saul and David was over. His external policies were based on *détente*, the fostering of political and economic ties with neighbouring states.

As was customary in a later age with the crowned heads of Europe, alliances were strengthened by convenient marriages. For Solomon, nuptual diplomacy was not subject to the restraints of monogamy. The foreign princesses he married augmented his already extensive harem, in itself an important status symbol for a king. At the same time the biblical statistic of seven hundred wives and three hundred concubines should be regarded as a flattering legend, not an authentic body-count. They included '. . . Moabite, Ammonite, Edomite, Sidonian and Hittite women. . . .' (I kings 11:1)

Solomon's most glittering matrimonial prize was the daughter of the Egyptian Pharaoh Siamun, the second-last ruler in the feeble twenty-first dynasty. As her dowry the Canaanite city of Gezer was ceded to Solomon – a gift that early biblical scholars found hard to explain. However, from archaeological evidence, it appears that Gezer and two or three other towns on the coastal plain were destroyed about the middle of the tenth century BC (that is, early in Solomon's reign) and were later rebuilt by Solomon. It is surmised that an Egyptian expeditionary force may have attempted to reassert control over the southern part of the country and then withdrawn. Egypt at that time lacked the power for expansion. Such an abortive thrust may explain the Pharaoh's willingness to conclude a political alliance with Solomon and seal it by marriage, together with the 'gift' of a key city that had been in temporary Egyptian occupation. As befitted her rank, Pharaoh's daughter and her retinue were given special quarters in the royal compound.

The foreign princesses were allowed to maintain their own pagan cults and shrines in Jerusalem. That the scriptural editors disapproved of this easy-going tolerance is shown by the irate tone of the text. Solomon's wives, it is written, '. . . turned away his heart after other gods; and his heart was not wholly true to the Lord his God, as was the heart of David his father'. (I Kings 11:4) The Lord's anger over this matter is suggested as the cause of the difficulties Solomon had with rebellious vassals in the latter part of his reign, and of the split in the kingdom after his death.

On the practical level, Solomon's closest and most rewarding alliance was with his father's associate, Hiram king of Tyre. The basis for the relationship was economic rather than political.

In bilateral trade the products of the two neighbouring states were complementary. The Israel agricultural economy had an exportable surplus of wheat and olive oil that Hiram needed. The Phoenician kingdom could supply Solomon's building projects with timber from the Lebanese mountains, minerals, skilled labour and technology. In international commerce they were natural partners.

The expansion under David had given the Israelite kingdom great geo-political advantages. It had become a 'two-ocean' country, with ports on the Mediterranean littoral and also at the tip of the Gulf of Aqaba that led to the Red Sea. Moreover, the kingdom lay astride the main caravan routes linking the Nile valley and the Arabian peninsula with Asia Minor and the Mesopotamian basin to the north and north-west.

The tolls on the caravans in transit was an important item in Solomon's revenues. In addition the king's commercial agents produced a lucrative income by handling the exchange of goods between countries to the north and the south. A striking example is given in the Bible. For his own army Solomon imported chariots manufactured in Egypt and horses bred in the Anatolian territory of Cilicia. Having developed these sources of supply the royal merchants became the middlemen for selling both horses and chariots to the Syrians.

The Phoenician domain ruled by Hiram was small, a coastal strip stretching northward from the gulf of Acre for little more than a hundred and sixty kilometres. The main port cities were Tyre, Sidon and Byblos. In Solomon's time Tyre was the dominant city and the virtual capital of Phoenicia, though the name Sidonians came to be used for Phoenicians in general.

The Phoenicians were remarkably skilled and enterprising. They were expert at a variety of arts and crafts: the extraction of the renowned purple dye from a species of mollusc found along their coast; cloth weaving; glass blowing; and the making of jewellery and handicrafts from ivory, metal, stone and glass. They were among the best builders and architects in the region. They developed a fishing industry – in fact they claimed to have invented it. Above all they were master sea-traders. The ships they constructed from their native timber plied westward along the chain of Mediterranean islands – Cyprus, Rhodes, Crete, Sicily, Sardinia and Corsica – and along the North African coast as far as Spain. Some of their trading stations were to develop into colonies. One of them, Carthage (near Tunis), later became an independent power challenging Rome.

The Phoenicians dealt not only in their home products but also carried to the West the spices and incense from Arabia and exotic birds and beasts from East Africa The ships returned loaded with iron and copper ore from their North African mines. A significant cargo spread by the Phoenician mariners was their Semitic alphabet, akin to that of Hebrew. It was from them that the Greeks learnt to write.

In the time of David and Solomon the Israelites welcomed cooperation with these useful neighbours. Afterwards they would rue the impact of Phoenician pagan deities on the Mosaic faith.

King Solomon and King Hiram went into partnership to open a trade route by sea from the southern Israelite port of Ezion-geber (near modern Eilat) into the Red Sea. With the help of Hiram's shipwrights, a small fleet of vessels was constructed at Ezion-geber. They were manned by mixed crews of Phoenician sailors and Israelites. Their main destination was the fabulous land of Ophir, from which fine gold was obtained. It was probably situated on the Red Sea coast of what is now Yemen. The first voyage brought back a large quantity of gold, also 'silver, ivory, apes and peacocks'. The round trip on these leisurely trade missions took about three years.

The Bible does not reveal what exports were carried from Ezion-geber as barter for the commodities brought home. There is reason to believe that among them was copper or copper ore mined at Timna, north of Eilat (where the present-day Israel copper plant is located) and in the Arava, the rift valley south of the Dead Sea. The wadis in these areas show evidence of copper extraction over thousands of years, with primitive smelting furnaces that used the strong desert winds as bellows. The vessels constructed for the Red Sea route are explicitly described as 'ships of Tarshish', a broad type designed by the Phoenicians for carrying ore from their mining ventures in the Mediterranean. (The word 'Tarshish' probably meant a metal-smelting plant and became the place-name of the farthest Phoenician enterprise of this kind, in southern Spain.)

THE QUEEN OF SHEBA

The royal visit to Solomon by the Queen of Sheba may have been connected with the southward push of the Israelites and Phoenician traders. Her small country probably lay on the Arabian coast towards the southern end of the Red Sea. Its people were energetic merchants handling the profitable commerce in the spices and incense produced in southern areas of Arabia. She had several motives for undertaking the arduous twenty-one-hundred-kilometre trek over deserts and mountains. One of them, no doubt, was curiosity to meet the monarch, reports of whose wealth and wisdom had spread through her part of the region. Other reasons were practical. The goods despatched by her merchants had to pass through Solomon's territory, and the transit arrangements could usefully be discussed. She may also have feared that the new sea route from Ezion-geber would cut into the overland traffic on which her people depended. (Two and a half millennia later, America would be discovered in the search for a maritime spice route to the East to bypass the ancient caravan roads.)

The queen arrived in great state with a large retinue and camels loaded with costly gifts: gold, precious stones and a massive consignment of spices. To test the renowned wisdom of her host, her baggage also included a series of 'cunning riddles' that Solomon answered with ease. Coming from a bleak corner of Arabia, she was unprepared for the style and splendour of Solomon's court: 'And when the queen of Sheba had seen all the wisdom of Solomon, the house that he had built, the food of his table, the seating of his officials, and the attendance of his

servants, their clothing, his cupbearers, and his burnt offerings which
he offered at the house of the Lord, there was no more spirit in her.'
(I Kings 10:4, 5) (The Hebrew word *ruach* can be translated as 'spirit'
or 'breath'. The expression in the above quotation 'there was no more
spirit in her', really meant that she was left breathless with amazement.)

The occasion was clearly a most cordial one on both sides, and presumably resulted in a good commercial understanding. There is no suggestion in the Bible that the encounter involved more than social and
business exchanges. The official mythology of Ethiopia would have it
otherwise. There it is believed that the kingdom of Sheba lay on the
African shore of the Red Sea, in what is today Somaliland; that after the
visit to the Israelite capital the queen bore Solomon a son, called Menelik, and that he founded a dynasty of Ethiopian rulers. For this reason
the emperors of Ethiopia, including the late Haile Selassie, used 'Lion
of Judah' as one of their official titles.

The luxury that so impressed the queen sprang from revenues that
flowed into the royal treasury from tribute payments, caravan tolls,
trading monopolies, the royal estates and the internal tax system.
The money flowed out again just as rapidly to finance costly building
projects.

Under David, Jerusalem had remained basically what it was when he
took it from the Jebusites. Solomon expanded and embellished it to
make a capital worthy of the prestige and prosperity acquired by the
Hebrew kingdom. The city limits were pushed up the slope of Mount
Moriah to its summit, doubling the area enclosed within the walls. By
levelling and filling a platform was created for the Temple and the surrounding compound. It included the threshing floor of Araunah acquired
by David. The palace and its complex of buildings were located on a
lower terrace.

The blocks of stone for these buildings were quarried in the nearby
hills and hauled to the site. The timber, mainly cedarwood, was supplied
by Hiram, king of Tyre, from the Lebanese forests. The logs were trans-
ported to the coast, floated in rafts to the port of Joppa, and from there
hauled up to Jerusalem.

Hiram also delivered a large amount of gold. That seems surprising,
as their joint venture brought quantities of gold from the land of Ophir
in the south. It may be that the voyages to the Red Sea took place at a
later stage in Solomon's reign. But in any case, as is clear from the text,
no single source of supply could have furnished all the gold used lavishly

for the decoration and implements of the Temple and in the furnishings of the palace. The latter included hundreds of ornamental shields, the great ivory throne inlaid with gold, and all the drinking vessels made of the precious metal – 'none [was] of silver, it was not considered as anything in the days of Solomon'. (I Kings 10:21)

Hiram's most essential contribution was the skilled Phoenician artisans – architects, masons, carpenters and metal workers. Solomon paid Hiram in wheat and oil, but the deficit became so large that in the end accounts were balanced by the cession to the Phoenicians of the Cabul district, inland from the bay of Acre, a strip of territory containing twenty villages.

The whole labour force involved in the Jerusalem projects was said to number eighty thousand men on the buildings and the stone quarries, and another ten thousand on the cutting and transport of the timber.

THE TEMPLE

The building of the Temple was started in the fourth year of Solomon's reign and completed in the eleventh year. No archaeological remains have been found, but it can be reconstructed from the details given in three Old Testament Books: I Kings, 2 Chronicles and Ezekiel. Its small dimensions and its proximity to the palace led some modern scholars to suggest that it was intended primarily as a royal chapel. However it did without doubt serve as a central sanctuary for the nation. The building itself was not meant as a synagogue in the modern sense, but as a dwelling for the *Shechinah*, the Divine Presence that hovered over the Ark of the Law. The congregation gathered in the courtyard outside, where the altar of sacrifices stood.

The Temple faced eastward towards the rising sun. The ground plan followed the pattern common at the time in the region. There were three chambers of equal width, one behind the other: the *Ulam* (vestibule); the *Hechal* (main hall); and the *Debir* (Holy of Holies) where the Ark rested between the four-metre winged creatures known as cherubim. Round the sides and back of the building was a double tier of smaller rooms used for storage, the robing of priests and so forth. The overall dimensions were about 50 metres (165 feet) in length, half that in width and 15 metres (50 feet) in height. The inside was panelled with carved cedarwood overlaid with gold. The courtyard was furnished with a group of monumental bronze works: two huge columns flanking the main entrance; a great bronze bowl of water, called the 'molten sea'; the main sacrificial altar in the form of four stepped tiers; and ten smaller layers for ceremonial ablutions by the priests.

The tribal elders and notables from all over the country gathered in Jerusalem for the dedication ceremony. To the sound of trumpets and cymbals the Ark was carried from David's tent to its new permanent abode. King Solomon blessed the crowd and knelt upon the altar in a prayer to the Lord. A great number of sacrifices and burnt offerings followed, and the inaugural feast lasted for seven days.

The beauty of the Temple and its superb craftsmanship made it one of the wonders of the ancient Near East, and added to the lustre of Solomon's reign. But its importance went far beyond its architecture. It gave tangible expression to the covenant God had made with David, giving the divine blessing to his dynasty, and therefore to the institution of kingship that was, for the Israelites, still new and in some quarters dubious. Its existence made Jerusalem not only the capital city but the Holy City. Long after the final destruction of the Temple, its memory would remain for a scattered people the symbol of their future Return.

After the completion of the Temple it took another thirteen years for Solomon to construct the palace complex. In addition to the royal quarters for the king and his wives, it contained a Judgement Hall holding the ivory throne, a public hall called the 'House of the Forest of Lebanon' because of its rows of cedar pillars, and other government buildings.

Outside the capital Solomon's building projects concentrated on ensuring external defence and internal security. The key projects were the 'cities for his chariots' (I Kings 9:19) at three strategic points: Hazor in north-eastern Galilee, commanding the road to Damascus; Megiddo, controlling the pass through the Carmel range into the valley of Jezreel; and Gezer, in the central coastal plain.

These three chariot cities had similar Solomonic fortifications – external walls of the casemate type (that is, double walls with chambers between them), and a gateway of striking design, flanked by twin towers behind which were three rooms on each side. Judging by a passage from Ezekiel (Ezekiel 40:6–10), the prototype for these gateways was one which led into the Temple compound in Jerusalem.

Archaeological excavations at the sites of all three chariot cities have confirmed that identical walls and gateways discovered there date from the period of Solomon. At Hazor the archaeologists dug down through twenty-one successive levels of settlement, the lowest from the Early Bronze Age 4500 years ago, and they came across Solomon's city at the tenth stratum from the surface. He had built his structures on a high bottle-shaped mound, the upper city of Hazor, some ten hectares in extent, as distinct from the seventy-hectare rectangular plateau below it to its immediate north, the lower city. The excavations bear out the biblical account that at the time of the Israelite conquest in the thirteenth century BC, Hazor was the leading Canaanite city-state in the north, 'the head of all those kingdoms', and that Joshua captured and burnt it. The archaeologists discovered its charred remains. After that the lower city had not been settled again, and life was renewed only on the mound. On its western half Solomon constructed a fortified citadel enclosed by a casemate wall. It contained a spacious residence for his military governor, public buildings and storerooms.

At Megiddo the most notable remains of Solomon's fortifications uncovered by the archaeologists are those of a casemate wall and a heavy gate with basalt door-sockets which had originally been lined with iron. Megiddo lies at the southern edge of the Jezreel valley, thirty-five kilometres south-east of modern Haifa. By controlling the nearby pass, it controlled the immemorial highway from Egypt to Mesopotamia at the point where it left the coastal plain and entered the Jezreel valley. At Megiddo, too, the spade of the archaeologist uncovered twenty layers of civilization, the first dating back to the Chalcolithic period in the fourth millennium BC. Its commanding position made it a frequent battleground throughout history. At this strategic spot the good king Josiah of Judah fell in combat against the Egyptian army in 609 BC. Napoleon's troops marched through here in 1799, and marched back in retreat three months later. Here, too, the British forces under Allenby broke through the Turkish defences in 1918. After bloody encounters for the possession of Megiddo over thousands of years, it is not surprising that the Book of Revelations in the New Testament predicts that the last battle of the world will be fought 'at a place called in the Hebrew tongue Armageddon', a corruption of Har Megiddon, the Mount of Megiddo.

At Hazor, with a history, like Megiddo, going back to the fourth millennium BC, the archaeologists also found at the tenth-century-BC level remains of the Solomonic city gate and parts of an adjacent casemate wall. As one of Solomon's main military bases, Gezer controlled the central coastal plain and the approach to Jerusalem from the west.

The horse-drawn chariot was the battle tank of ancient times. It required advanced industrial technology to have been produced in the early Iron Age, and superior military organization to maintain and operate chariot squadrons on a substantial scale. Before David the Israelites had not acquired chariots nor learnt to use them. Anyway, they lived in the hills, which were suitable terrain for foot soldiers but not for chariots. In Deborah's celebrated battle in the Jezreel valley the chariots of the Canaanite general Sisera got stuck in the mud, and the Israelite highlanders then charged down on them from the slope above. David's army may have included a small number of chariots, though that is uncertain. The king himself would move round in the city in a chariot, with runners clearing the street for him, and it was this royal prerogative that Absalom exercised when he made his bid for power, as Adonijah would later do.

It was Solomon who built up important chariot forces, keeping part of them in Jerusalem and concentrating the rest at Hazor, Megiddo and Gezer. Conflicting figures are given in different biblical passages about the total strength of these forces. One estimate puts them at fourteen hundred chariots, with a complement of three horses for each, while another more conservative suggestion is that there were five hundred.

A number of other strong-points and 'store cities' constructed by Solomon have been excavated, some of them not mentioned in the Bible. Marking them on a map one sees that they form a carefully designed network that enabled Solomon to protect the heartland of the Israelite tribes, control the highways and the passes through the hills, and subdue restless vassals. Although Solomon was not a warrior king like his father David, he had an excellent grasp of security needs, and maintained a high level of military force skilfully dispersed at all strategic points. As a shrewd and realistic ruler, he did not believe that foreign alliances were a substitute for self-defence, or that peace could rest on weakness.

On the surface, conditions in the kingdom appeared idyllic.

Judah and Israel were as many as the sand by the sea; they ate and drank and were happy. Solomon ruled over all the kingdoms from the Euphrates to the land of the Philistines and to the border of Egypt . . . and he had peace on all sides round about him. And Judah and Israel dwelt in safety, from Dan even to Beersheba, every man under his vine and under his fig tree, all the days of Solomon. [I Kings 4:20–1, 24–5]

It is estimated that in the less than eighty years spanned by the reigns of David and Solomon, the Israelite population doubled itself, according to the renowned biblical scholar Professor W. F. Albright, from about four hundred thousand to about eight hundred thousand. The towns grew in size and number and the general standard of living rose – for instance, the four-roomed stone house became the common family unit at this time. Imported luxury goods were in common use. The level of culture and technology visibly improved to a large extent under the influence of more sophisticated neighbours like the Egyptians and the Phoenicians.

Yet in spite of the general progress cracks began to show in the edifice of the State during the latter part of Solomon's reign. The royal coffers were constantly emptied by the extravagance of the court and by Solomon's ambitious building programmes. As a result the burdens on the population increased, and discontent was fed by tribal anger.

Solomon had carried out a reorganization of the kingdom into twelve districts administered by commissioners appointed by and responsible to the king. This reform had its own bureaucratic validity. It streamlined local government and brought it under central direction. At the same time the Israelite territories and the annexed Canaanite enclaves were brought into a single administrative framework. But there was a backlash of resentment to the change. The district lines in certain areas cut across the old tribal boundaries, and the powers of the district commissioners robbed the tribal leaders of what authority they had left.

The system of districts was made the basis for a novel form of taxation in kind. Each commissioner had to raise enough food-stuffs to supply the palace in Jerusalem for one month a year. That this was no small exaction appears from the list of daily requirements given in the text – 'thirty cors of fine flour, and sixty cors of meal, ten fat oxen, and twenty pasture-fed cattle, a hundred sheep, besides harts, gazelles, roebucks, and fatted fowl'. (I Kings 4:22, 23) (A 'cor' is over six US bushels.) It has been calculated that these quantities could provide a gourmet table for a royal establishment of five to six thousand persons. The districts also had to provide fodder for all the king's horses in the country. The twelve districts covered 'all Israel', a term which did not include Judah. That home tribe of David's dynasty was put in a favoured position. It came directly under a senior official at the court, and was exempted from the food tax. A sense of discrimination pervaded the northern tribes, and the seeds of schism began to sprout again.

The problem of finding enough workers for construction projects led to an extremely unpopular measure, the *corvée*, or forced labour. The Bible is ambivalent on this issue. It is said in one passage that Solomon made 'a forced levy of slaves' from the Canaanite peoples that had been absorbed into the kingdom. 'But of the people of Israel Solomon made no slaves; they were the soldiers, they were his officials, his commanders, his captains, his chariot commanders and his horsemen.' (I Kings 9:22) Yet it appears from other references that the distinction between military service for Israelites and civilian forced labour for non-Israelites was not maintained in practice. Elsewhere it is plainly stated that thirty thousand forced labourers were raised out of 'all Israel', and that they were sent in rotation to do the tree cutting in Lebanon, ten thousand at a time for one month out of three. Moreover, we learn that Solomon was impressed by the ability of a young man from Ephraim called Jeroboam, and put him in charge of all the 'forced labour of the house of Joseph' at work on ground levelling in Jerusalem. (The House of Joseph meant the tribes of Ephraim and Manasseh that occupied the central hill-country.) Ephraim was the largest and most important of the northern tribes, and during the period of the Judges had held the central sanctuary at Shiloh. It was jealous of Judah's predominant position under the united monarchy and resentful of the concentration in Jerusalem of all the powers of government.

Jeroboam led a revolt against Solomon, encouraged by a prophet called Ahijah who came from Shiloh. A meeting between the two men on the road from Jerusalem personified two sources of opposition to Solomon, the northern tribes and the ultra-orthodox religious circles, who were outraged by the pagan practices permitted at the court. Ahijah predicted the secession of ten tribes under Jeroboam, and illustrated his prophecy by tearing his new garment into pieces. The revolt was quickly suppressed and Jeroboam fled for his life to Egypt. Solomon may have dismissed this episode as of little consequence, but its message was clear and ominous.

Solomon's later years saw signs that the royal authority was eroding in the vassal states as well. There was an attempted rebellion in Edom, led by Hadad, a member of the Edomite royal family who had been taken to Egypt as a child when David conquered that territory. In the north the kingdom of Aram-Damascus cast off Jerusalem's sway and regained its independence under King Rezom.

The cumulative strains were held in check by the king's ability and prestige. When he died, they tore the kingdom apart.

Solomon emerges from the biblical record as a less appealing figure than his father. There is little in his story to match the drama and human interest of the Bethlehem shepherd boy's rise to power. Solomon was born a royal prince and the succession had been secured for him by his mother and a faction of David's courtiers. Once on the throne, he brought redoubtable gifts to the task: a keen intellect, organizing ability, diplomatic talents and a zeal for building rivalled in Jewish history only by Herod the Great nine centuries later. But compared to David, his personality appears aloof, distant and lacking in warmth.

He was, claims the Bible, 'wiser than other men'. He was said to have composed three thousand proverbs and a thousand and five songs. His accomplishments included great erudition about the flora and fauna of the region. He could discourse on 'trees, from the cedar that is in Lebanon to the hyssop that grows out of the wall; he spoke also of beasts, and of birds, and of reptiles, and of fish'. (I Kings 4:33)

In the ancient cultures of the Near East, *chochmah* (wisdom) was an attribute much admired but hard to define. It originated in folk wisdom – the practical philosophy of everyday life expressed in proverbs, parables, fables, riddles and poems. Among the educated classes these traditional forms became a test of intellectual and literary skills, and collections of maxims gained wide currency.

Given Solomon's renown as a sage, it was natural that he should be regarded as the father of the Hebrew genre known as Wisdom Literature, just as the religious laws and precepts were identified with Moses and the psalms with David. There are three 'Wisdom Books' in the Old Testament – Proverbs, Job and Ecclesiastes – and two more were included among the Apocrypha in the Christian Bible: The Wisdom of Solomon, and the Wisdom of Ben Sirah, also known as Ecclesticus. Three of these five works are ascribed to the authorship of Solomon: Proverbs, Ecclesiastes and The Wisdom of Solomon. In the case of the last two, the attribution is no more than a literary fiction. Ecclesiastes appears to have been written by a pessimistic and highly sceptical Jewish intellectual of the third century BC, during the Hellenistic period and before the Maccabean revolt. The Wisdom of Solomon is a book in praise of traditional Hebrew wisdom, written in Greek in the first century BC by an unknown Alexandrian Jew.

The biblical Book of Proverbs is of much more ancient origin, and comprises several collections made at different times. The largest collection is simply called 'The Proverbs of Solomon'; the next largest bears the heading 'Proverbs of Solomon, which the men of Hezekiah, King of Judah, copied out'. These maxims may well have originated in Solomon's time or even earlier, and a number of them could in theory have been composed by him and the elite at his court.

On the whole their impact is stronger in the Hebrew original than in English translation. Hebrew is an extremely pithy language, and in the Book of Proverbs the *mashal* (proverb) has a standardized form – a sentence of six to eight words, with a balance between the first and second parts. The content does not emphasize spiritual qualities or theological concepts, but the everyday virtues that promote a successful life and the respect of one's fellowmen: industry, thrift, piety, moderation, honesty, charity and tolerance. These qualities add up to what the Jewish sages call *chochmat chaim* (the wisdom of living). Its parallel is known in the western world as the Protestant ethic.

Of an entirely different character is the Song of Solomon – or, to give its full title, 'The Song of Songs, which is Solomon's'. Its traditional attribution can be rationalized only on the flimsy grounds that he wrote songs and had many wives. However his alleged authorship brought about the strange inclusion in the Bible of a series of rich and sensual love poems lacking any overt religious content.

The songs appear to have been designed for singing by the bride and bridegroom at a wedding celebration. To justify its scriptural status the Jewish sages interpreted the work as an allegorical dialogue between God and his chosen people, while Christian theologians saw in the bridegroom and bride an allegory for Jesus and the Church.

PART TWO

THE TWO KINGDOMS

6

The Split

The solid-looking United Kingdom had taken a century to construct, during the reigns of Saul, David and Solomon. With the death of Solomon in 922 BC the edifice fell apart overnight. Two second-rate rump kingdoms were left, bickering with one another and exposed to external pressure.

Judah, the southern kingdom, retained most of the territory of Benjamin along its northern border, thus safeguarding Jerusalem. The tribe of Simeon in the Beersheba area in the south had already been absorbed into Judah and lost its separate identity. The southern kingdom was the smaller and poorer of the two, and more withdrawn from the affairs of the region. It remained stable internally, loyal to the Davidic dynasty, and with Jerusalem and the Temple as the permanent focus of its national and religious life. Judah was to survive almost three and a half centuries until the destruction of Jerusalem by a Babylonian army in 587 BC.

Israel, the northern kingdom, comprised the other nine Israelite tribes (or ten, counting part of Benjamin) in the hill-country, the coastal area, the Galilee and Trans-jordan. It was larger in area and population than Judah, and more prosperous because of its fertile soil and the major trade routes that passed through it. Israel was in the mainstream of regional events and involved with neighbouring states – whether friendly like the Phoenicians or hostile like Aram-Damascus to the north-east. Compared to Judah, Israel was unstable since it lacked internal cohesion and never developed a durable royal dynasty. Nor did it acquire a capital and a central sanctuary with the appeal of Jerusalem and the Temple. Israel lasted over two centuries, and came to an end with the Assyrian capture of Samaria in 722 BC.

The separatist tendencies among the northern tribes had been firmly suppressed by Solomon. They welled up against his son and successor

75

Rehoboam (922–915 BC), whose mother was the Ammonite princess Naamah. Forty-one years old at his accession, he lacked the force of personality and the political skills of his father and grandfather.

Rehoboam's acceptance by Judah presented no problems. But the northern tribes refused to have their allegiance taken for granted. The new king was obliged to travel to Shechem, the leading city in the north, and to appear there before an assembly of tribal elders. They were in an intractable mood, and bluntly stated their grievances and demands concerning taxes, forced labour and other exactions under Solomon. 'Your father made our yoke heavy. Now therefore lighten the hard service of your father and his heavy yoke upon us, and we will serve you.' (I Kings 12:4) Rehoboam asked for three days to consider their petition, and consulted his counsellors. The older men who had been with his father urged him to conciliate the northern leaders, and to 'speak good words to them'. Rehoboam, however, was swayed by the cocky young men of his own age group. When the tribal elders reconvened, he rudely rebuffed them, in the mistaken belief that tough language would be construed as a show of strength. 'My father made your yoke heavy, but I will add to your yoke; my father chastised you with whips, but I will chastise you with scorpions.' (I Kings 12:14)

That was the breaking point. The Israel notables once more raised the secessionist cry of Sheba, the son of Bichri, when he had tried to rebel against David half a century earlier: 'What portion have we in David? We have no inheritance in the son of Jesse. To your tents, O Israel!' (I Kings 12:16)

Rehoboam and his retinue hurriedly withdrew from this uproar, and Adoram, the official in charge of forced labour, was sent to restore order. That was a remarkably inept thing to do, as no royal officer could have been more detested. Adoram was stoned to death by the crowd; Rehoboam jumped into his chariot and fled back to Jerusalem.

In Egypt, the dynasty connected by marriage to Solomon had been swept away by the vigorous Libyan officer Shishak, who seized the throne and established the twenty-second dynasty.

When Jeroboam fled to Egypt after his abortive revolt against Solomon, he was given political asylum by Shishak who saw in him a potential instrument for undermining the Israelite kingdom and regaining Egyptian influence.

On hearing of Solomon's death Jeroboam had returned to his home in

Ephraim, and had emerged as the leading spokesman in the fateful meetings with Rehoboam in Shechem. The assembly of tribal elders now set up the independent kingdom of Israel and elected Jeroboam as its first king (922–901 BC). He established his capital in Shechem, the tribal centre of Ephraim. Jeroboam later moved the capital to the former Canaanite city and strategic road junction of Tirzah, eleven kilometres north-east of Shechem.

The secession of the north nearly led to a bitter and bloody civil war. Back in Jerusalem Rehoboam would not accept the partition of the country as an accomplished fact. He mustered the fighting men of Judah and Benjamin and planned to march northward and restore union by force. However, he was dissuaded from this rash course by Shemaiah, at that time the most influential prophetic figure in Jerusalem, who declared flatly in the name of the Lord, 'You shall not go up or fight against your kinsmen, the people of Israel. Return every man to his home . . .' (I Kings 12:24)

There were objective reasons why Rehoboam would have been ill-advised to embark on a long and costly military adventure. The text implies that he had to rely on the local militia in Judah, because the formidable regular army built up by David and Solomon would not have been available to him for the prosecution of a civil war. Both the loyalties and the deployment of the armed forces were divided between the two kingdoms. The important 'chariot cities' of Hazor and Megiddo, and possibly Gezer, fell within the northern kingdom. Furthermore, Judah was impoverished, having lost the main sources of revenue of the United Kingdom: tribute from vassals; control of the commercial arteries; foreign trade; and the taxes from the northern tribes.

Five years after the split Pharaoh Shishak swept through and plundered both Hebrew kingdoms. Entering by the coastal route through Gaza, he took control of Philistia and marched inland on Jerusalem. Rehoboam averted an assault by buying Shishak off with heavy tribute, including the Temple treasures and the shields of beaten gold with which Solomon had lined the palace walls. Rehoboam sadly replaced the precious heirloom with shields of bronze. Even without the bribe it is doubtful whether Shishak would have wanted to lay siege to Jerusalem in the course of a swift expedition through the country.

The Bible is silent about the rest of the Egyptian campaign, but it can be reconstructed from the list of places Shishak had inscribed on a temple wall at Karnak in Upper Egypt. It appears that from Jerusalem, he struck northward into the kingdom of Israel. His troops crossed the River Jordan to Mahanaim, continued northward and back across the river at Beth-shan, headed westward through the valley of Jezreel and came down the coastal plain on their way back to Egypt. One force branched off at the beginning of the campaign and raided the Negev, cutting across to Arad, then down to the Dead Sea and along the Aravah to Ezion-geber. The destruction of the port buildings there put an end to hopes of reviving the lucrative sea route to the south that had lapsed at the end of Solomon's reign. Archaeological evidence supports Shishak's claim that he ravaged a number of fortified cities and strongholds along his route, including Megiddo and Gezer. A fragment of a Shishak stele has been found at Megiddo.

Faithful to its own angle of vision, the Bible attributes Shishak's campaign to the Lord's anger with Rehoboam and the people of Judah for sinful conduct, such as frequenting pagan hill-shrines and tolerating a cult of male prostitutes. Jerusalem was spared only because the king and his nobles showed humility and repentance. However, Rehoboam took a more mundane view of the threat to the kingdom. In the Book of Chronicles fifteen towns are listed in southern Judah that were fortified by him. The strongholds were provided with adequate reserves of food and weapons, and were linked by a network of internal roads. It is unclear whether this defence programme was initiated in advance of Shishak's campaign. During Rehoboam's reign no effort was made to fortify the northern border with the kingdom of Israel, the scene of intermittent local clashes. Rehoboam was unwilling to recognize the separate existence of the northern kingdom, or to accept the frontier as permanent.

By the standards of his father Solomon, Rehoboam had a modest domestic establishment, only eighteen wives and sixty concubines, who bore him twenty-eight sons and sixty daughters. His favourite wife was his kinswoman Maacah, the daughter of Absalom. Her eldest son, Abijah, was made the crown prince. A number of the other princes were appointed to posts in the provinces '. . . and he gave them abundant provisions, and procured wives for them'. (II Chronicles 11:23) Rehoboam was succeeded by Abijah (915–913 BC).

THE REIGN OF JEROBOAM – (Northern Kingdom)

Returning to the Northern Kingdom we realize that Jeroboam must have been a man of commanding presence and outstanding leadership qualities to have been the unanimous choice of the northern tribes as their ruler. After all, he had no dynastic claim and no known advantage of rank or wealth. It may be that the courage he had shown as a young man in standing up to the mighty Solomon had made his name renowned among the northern tribes, certainly in his own tribe of Ephraim. But since that episode he had spent years in Egyptian exile and it was a tribute to the impression he made that on his return he took the lead in the protest at Shechem, before the final break with Rehoboam. In the minds of the tribal elders there may also have been the thought that Jeroboam was a protégé of the Pharaoh Shishak, and help might be forthcoming from that quarter if Rehoboam should invade.

It is of interest that the appointment of Jeroboam followed the old charismatic tradition of the Judges that had been the basis for Saul's mandate. The prophet Ahijah performed the role of Samuel as a nominating instrument on behalf of the Lord. The democratic machinery of an electoral college of tribal leaders then came into play.

Jeroboam needed all his capacity to face the formidable task of establishing a separate kingdom and creating its political, administrative and religious institutions. Fortunately the disintegration of the United Kingdom stopped short with its split into two. There was no serious attempt to restore the old pre-Saul order when the tribes (with the possible exception of Judah) were held together in a loose covenant league, and each was master in its own territory. Israelite society had undergone fundamental changes during the previous century. The institution of kingship had taken root. The overall power of the throne; administration through a state bureaucracy; a professional army; the drift from the rural areas to the cities; the emergence of new economic classes (landowners, merchants and skilled artisans); the decline of local shrines and the prestige of the Temple and its priesthood – all these factors had whittled away authority at the tribal level. The households, clans and tribes still remained the carriers of social tradition and kinship ties, but were no longer power-centres. Thus it was that the seceding northern tribes did not revert to their old autonomy but remained together in a single union, and retained kingship as their collective form of government. However much nostalgia there was in the air, the clock could not be turned back to the days of the Judges.

The name 'Israel' had powerful associations with the Hebrew past and therefore gave the new kingdom a feeling of continuity. It was the name acquired by Jacob, the common ancestor of all the tribes, after he had wrestled with the angel at the ford of Jabbok. The freed slaves who followed Moses out of Egypt were the *Bnai Yisrael* (Children of Israel), and the area they settled in Canaan was *Eretz Yisrael* (the Land of Israel). It is possible that the realm of David and Solomon had been called the Kingdom of Israel, though that is not explicitly stated in the Bible and remains obscure. If that were so, retaining the name after the split would have fortified a claim of legitimacy for the northern kingdom. After its destruction nearly twenty-eight centuries would pass before a state called Israel would once again appear on the map of the region.

David had ensured that both secular and religious authority were vested in his throne, and that the centre of both was in Jerusalem. Jeroboam saw clearly that the political independence of the new kingdom could not be sustained unless there was a religious break as well. '. . . if this people go up to offer sacrifices in the house of the Lord at Jerusalem, then the heart of this people will turn again to their Lord, to Rehoboam king of Judah, and they will kill me and return to Rehoboam king of Judah'. (I Kings 12:27)

As a counter-attraction to the Temple, Jeroboam revived the use of two ancient sanctuaries and gave them royal status. One was Bethel, sixteen kilometres north of Jerusalem on the road to Shechem and close to the border of the two kingdoms. Bethel is mentioned in the Bible more often than any other place in the country except Jerusalem. It was a Canaanite town from about the twenty-first century BC. Abraham built an altar to the Lord close by, on his first visit to the land of Canaan. Here Jacob had his famous dream in which he saw a ladder reaching to heaven with angels going up and down it, and he gave the place the name of Bethel, 'House of God'. (Its Canaanite name was Luz.) The archaeological dig on the site indicates that the town was captured and burnt by Joshua at the time of the Conquest, and then resettled by Israelites. The Tabernacle and the Ark remained at Bethel for some time before a sanctuary was built at Shiloh, fifteen kilometres farther to the north. The prophetess Deborah lived near Bethel, and the prophet Samuel visited it regularly on his judicial circuit. The place Jeroboam chose as the religious centre for the southern part of his kingdom was therefore hallowed by many centuries of Hebrew history.

The other royal temple was at Dan, at the extreme north-eastern corner of the country near the foot of Mount Hermon and the sources of the River Jordan. It was a Canaanite city called Laish (also known in the Bible as Leshem), inhabited by a people connected with the Phoenicians of Sidon on the coast, and first mentioned in Egyptian sources in the eighteenth century BC. When the tribe of Dan was being squeezed by the Philistines out of the area in the Shephelah (lowlands) originally allotted to them, they captured Laish and migrated to that locality. The town was rebuilt and given the name of Dan, and a shrine was established, served by a young priest, and a graven image used that the Danites had 'collected' along the way from a farmer in Ephraim called Micah. The northern sanctuary selected by Jeroboam thus had an Israelite background dating back to the early period of the Judges.

In 1966 digging was begun at Tel Dan, also known by the Arabic name of Tel-el-Khadi (The Hill of the Judge). The site is on the Lebanese border where underground springs bubble up to form a lush green oasis, and flow off as the Dan river, one of the headwaters of the Jordan. A monumental gateway with a section of a broad processional street have been revealed dating from the early period of the Kingdom of Israel. Nearby is a *bamah* (high place) where a golden calf was placed in a temple built of ashlar blocks of stone, with a courtyard surrounding it. The archaeological evidence bears out the destruction of the Canaanite city by the Danites, and indicates that the sanctuary established by Jeroboam was further developed by Ahab when he became King.

Jeroboam placed a golden image of a calf in each of the two sanctuaries, which the Bible presents as plain idolatry. It quotes him as saying to the people: 'You have gone up to Jerusalem long enough. Behold your gods, O Israel, who brought you up out of the land of Egypt.' (I Kings 12:28) This charge is probably unjust and may reflect the bias of Jerusalem scribes against the northern kingdom. To them, Jeroboam's repudiation of the Davidic line together with the Temple made him both a rebel and a heretic. Modern scholars consider that the golden calves were meant as an equivalent to the cherubim in the Holy of Holies of the Temple – that is, as a footstool or throne over which hovered the invisible Shechinah, the Divine Presence. The traditions of the Sinai Covenant and the Mosaic Code were no less powerful among the northern tribes than in Judah, and a sudden switch to idol worship as the official cult is inconceivable. Bull symbols were not in themselves taboo in Hebrew religious practice. For instance, the great bronze basin known as the 'molten sea' in front of the Jerusalem Temple rested on the backs of twelve bronze oxen. Nevertheless Jeroboam's action may have been unwise and easily misinterpreted. Images of bulls and calves in pagan contexts were all too familiar throughout the Near East. The worship of the golden calf while Moses was up on Mount Sinai showed that the Children of Israel had carried with them from Egypt the cult of the bull-god Apis which had its centre at the ancient capital of Memphis. Among the Canaanite peoples bulls were commonly associated with fertility cults. Their appearance in Israelite sanctuaries was bound to offend orthodox circles.

Jeroboam's treatment of the Levites further antagonized the religious establishment. The tribe of Levi was unlike any of the others, in that its main function was to service the faith. The priesthood was by tradition appointed from certain Levite families that claimed descent from Aaron, the first High Priest. The rest of the Levites performed all the ritual chores except the most sacred tasks reserved for priests. After Joshua's conquest no specific territory was allotted to the tribe of Levi. Instead they were to be settled in forty-eight Levitical cities distributed among the other twelve tribes. Many scholars doubt whether this design became a reality, and believe that the rural priests and Levites were scattered wherever there were Israelite settlements.

During the reigns of David and Solomon, the Levites became in effect civil servants, carrying out various administrative duties for the monarchy in addition to their religious ones. They were appointed 'for all the work of the Lord and for the service of the king'. (I Chronicles 26:30) Assuming that they would remain loyal to the House of David and to the Temple, Jeroboam expelled all the priests and Levites from the northern kingdom, and they went to live in Judah. In their place Jeroboam appointed non-Levite priests from among the local population to serve at the two main sanctuaries and at the scattered hill-shrines.

A further separatist measure taken by Jeroboam was to change the date of *Succot* (the Feast of Booths) from the seventh month to the eighth month. Succot was the main harvest festival, when people from all over the country would go up to Jerusalem in pilgrimage and take part in the Temple services. Jeroboam sought to disrupt this practice in favour of Bethel and Dan.

The alienation by Jeroboam of conservative religious elements is illustrated by two stories told in the Bible at some length. The first concerns an unnamed old 'man of God' from Judah who suddenly appeared in the Bethel sanctuary and condemned Jeroboam, who was about to burn incense upon the altar. The outstretched arm of the irate king was paralysed and was restored only when Jeroboam expressed repentance. As a sign of disapproval from the Lord the altar broke into pieces and the ashes on it were scattered. When Jeroboam invited the eerie visitor to come home with him and have a meal, the old man refused firmly, saying that God had forbidden him to have food or drink in Bethel, and he went his way.

A local prophet hurried after him and deceived him into accepting hospitality. As a punishment the man of God was killed by a lion on his return journey, though miraculously the lion remained next to the body without eating it or harming the ass on which the old man had been riding. The contrite local prophet retrieved the corpse and buried it in his own family tomb. This strange tale has the marks of ancient origin; it is used here to express scriptural disapproval of Jeroboam's policies.

A turn of events more serious was that Ahijah, the prophetic sponsor of Jeroboam's kingship, now turned against him, much as Samuel had turned against Saul. Jeroboam's infant son was taken ill and he sent the mother to Shiloh to consult Ahijah, now aged and nearly blind. Jeroboam must already have been aware that Ahijah's attitude towards him had changed, because he instructed his wife to disguise herself and pretend to be someone else. However Ahijah knew at once who she was, having been told by the Lord to expect the visit. The prophet not only told her that the child would die, but took the opportunity to denounce Jeroboam for doing evil and predicted a dire fate for his descendants: the Lord will '. . . utterly consume the house of Jeroboam, as a man burns up dung until it is all gone. Any one belonging to Jeroboam who dies in the city the dogs shall eat; and any one who dies in the open country the birds of the air shall eat . . .' (I Kings 14:10–11)

With the division of David's empire after the death of Solomon, the kingdoms of Ammon and Moab appear to have thrown off the Israelite yoke. Aram-Damascus had successfully rebelled during Solomon's reign and drew into its orbit the other small Aramean states in southern Syria. Jeroboam however retained control of all the Israelite territories east of the Jordan river, from the Sea of Galilee down to the Dead Sea.

At the beginning of his reign, he had strengthened his hold in Trans-jordan by fortifying the town of Penuel in Gilead, on the King's Highway.

Jeroboam reigned for twenty-two years and was succeeded for a brief period by his son Nadab (901–900 BC). Fighting broke out on the Israel–Philistine border, and Nadab laid siege to the town of Gibbethon, west of Gezer. It had been one of the Levitical cities during the United Monarchy and had been regained by the Philistines. During the siege Nadab was murdered by Baasha, from the tribe of Issachar, probably one of his army officers. Baasha seized power, had himself proclaimed king in Tirzah, and promptly liquidated all the male descendants of Jeroboam. This was the first of a number of occasions when the throne of the northern kingdom changed hands through coup and assassination. (It is a melancholy reflection that in the world of the twentieth century, nearly three millennia after Baasha, regimes are changed by the bullet as often as by the ballot.) The accession of Baasha (900–877 BC) was a political turning-point in another sense – it broke the hegemony of the tribe of Ephraim in the affairs of the kingdom of Israel.

JUDAH UNDER ASA

Before the end of Jeroboam's reign King Abijah of Judah had extended the hold of the southern kingdom over disputed and strategically important territory in Benjamin, to the north of Jerusalem. He had occupied and annexed Bethel and the surrounding hills and towns. Abijah was succeeded after his short reign by his son Asa (913–873 BC). In the early part of the latter's reign, Baasha of Israel pushed south, having first secured good relations with Ben-hadad, the king of Aram-Damascus. Baasha regained the Bethel area that had been taken by Judah and advanced to Ramah, which he began to fortify. Ramah was only ten kilometres from Jerusalem, and commanded the road out of the capital to the north. Alarmed by this threat to Jerusalem and lacking the military strength to repulse the northern army, Asa sought outside help. He sent messengers to Ben-hadad in Damascus, who carried with them the gold and silver in the treasuries of the Temple and the palace, as a bribe to the Syrian king to switch sides and force Baasha to withdraw. Ben-hadad seized this opening to invade Israel from the north-east, and temporarily occupied the whole upper Jordan valley up to the Sea of Galilee. Baasha marched back hurriedly to deal with this attack in the rear. Asa's desperate call for the opening of a second front had achieved its purpose, but it set a dangerous precedent. From then on the Syrian neighbour was to play a significant role in the affairs of the Hebrew kingdoms.

Asa used the timber and stone captured at Ramah to fortify the nearby towns of Mizpah and Geber, thereby protecting Jerusalem from the north. In so doing he accepted what his grandfather Rehoboam had refused to accept, namely, that the division into two kingdoms was a fact. The border between them, as settled in the short war between Baasha and Asa, remained unchanged for the rest of the existence of the northern kingdom.

Judah, too, faced a sudden attack from the rear. A force under Zerah the Cushite (Ethiopian) came out of the Sinai desert and advanced through Philistia as far as Mareshah in the Shefelah, the Judean foot-hills. The army of Judah under Asa defeated Zerah's troops and pursued them southward to Gerar in Philistine territory, which was sacked and plundered, as was the surrounding countryside, with the capture of large flocks of sheep and herds of camels. According to the Book of Chronicles, Zerah's army was made up of Ethiopians and Libyans. Some scholars identify him as the Pharaoh Osorkon I, son of Shishak who had founded the twenty-second dynasty. Another theory is that he was an Ethiopian officer in command of the Egyptian forces in the Sinai. A third suggestion is that he was the leader of a community of Ethiopians who had settled in the Sinai with the indigenous nomad tribes.

Asa was a minor when he succeeded to the throne of Judah, and Maacah, the Ammonite widow of Rehoboam, acted as regent. (There is some textual confusion as to whether she was Asa's mother or grand-mother.) When Asa reached manhood he was determined to stamp out the pagan practices that had been fostered by Maacah. His first step was to remove the queen-mother from the regency, oust her supporters and publicly burn in the Kidron valley an image she had used in the worship of the Canaanite fertility goddess Asherah (Astarte). The practice of sacred prostitution was abolished and idols were destroyed throughout Judah, though the local 'high places' remained in use. Asa replenished the depleted Temple treasury with large endowments of gold and silver. In the fifteenth year of his reign he called to Jerusalem a convocation of leading men from all over the kingdom. It turned into a mass revivalist meeting; a great number of sacrifices were offered on the rebuilt Temple altar, and renewed oaths of devotion to God were taken 'with shouting, and with trumpets, and with horns'.

In the latter part of his reign Asa's religious zeal failed to satisfy the ultra-orthodox. They objected to the fact that he had appealed for help to the king of Damascus rather than to the Lord when threatened by the incursion of Baasha, the king of Israel. The zealots were further offended when Asa called in physicians, instead of relying on prayer, for a disease of the feet (probably dropsy) which caused him great suffering in the last two years of his life. Talmudic sages afterwards maintained that he was afflicted because he conscripted religious students and newly wed young men for army service. The disease must have caused rapid decomposition after death, since we are pointedly told that the royal body was laid out ' . . . on a bier which had been filled with various kinds of spices prepared by the perfumer's art'. (II Chronicles 16:14)

JUDAH UNDER JEHOSHAPHAT

Asa's lengthy reign of forty-one years was followed by that of his son Jehoshaphat (873–849 BC), the two of them together occupying the throne for sixty-six years. Jehoshaphat was a sensible energetic and pious ruler under whom Judah recovered much of its peace and prosperity.

Jehoshaphat accepted that the division into two Hebrew kingdoms was an irreversible fact, and sought peaceful cooperation between them, with a common front against external enemies. Since this attitude was shared by Ahab, the king of Israel, an alliance was concluded, and buttressed by the marriage of Jehoshaphat's crown prince, Jehoram, to the princess Athalia of Israel. It is uncertain whether she was Ahab's sister or his daughter by Queen Jezebel. During this period Judah joined forces with Israel in two military campaigns – an attack on the Syrian army of Aram-Damascus at Ramoth-gilead, where Ahab was killed, and an operation against Moab in the reign of Ahab's son.

Towards the end of Jehoshaphat's reign there was an incursion into Judah by a mixed force from three Trans-jordan kingdoms: Ammon, Moab and the rugged Mount Seir region of Edom, south-east of the Dead Sea. The force crossed the Dead Sea (probably at its narrow waist opposite Masada), came along the western shore to En-gedi and from there toiled up the steep escarpment of the Judean wilderness by the ascent of Ziz, penetrating into the Hebron hills. It was presumably repulsed or wiped out. There is no mention of this incident in any non-Biblical source, and it could not have been a large expedition. Some scholars surmise that the remains of forts on the high ground overlooking the Dead Sea in this area may indicate an attempt to stop the infiltration of bands across the water. The account in II Chronicles (Chapter 20) appears to be highly imaginative and more in the nature of a didactic parallel. It refers to the enemy force as a great multitude, and depicts an assembly in the Temple from all over Judah praying to the Lord for deliverance. A Levite inspired by God urges them to march towards the enemy in the Wilderness of Tekoa, south of Hebron, and they do so, with the singing Temple choir in the lead. The Lord causes the invaders to turn and slay one another. When the Israelites reach the spot they find piles of corpses and masses of booty that take three days to collect. The moral of the Chronicler is that prayer is a more potent weapon than arms, and that Jehoshaphat was awarded a victory without fighting for it because he relied on the Lord.

Jehoshaphat carried out a programme of internal reorganization in order to strengthen the institutions of the truncated southern kingdom. The army was grouped under five district commanders, three in Judah and two in the integrated territory of Benjamin. More work was carried out on the fortification of key cities and the chariot forces and army depots were dispersed among them. Relieved of concern about the security of the northern border with Israel, Jehoshaphat was thus able to impress his other neighbours by adopting a strong military posture. Philistia resumed the payment of tribute, and Judah also received gifts of livestock from 'the Arabs', presumably the nomadic desert tribes to the south.

Jehoshaphat strengthened the tenuous hold Judah had retained over Edomite territory in the Negev, and regained secure access to the southern port of Ezion-geber. An attempt was made to renew the trade route to the south for gold from Ophir and spices from Arabia. As a joint venture between Judah and Israel 'ships of Tarshish' were built at Ezion-geber but they foundered at sea in a storm.

Jehoshaphat continued the purge of pagan practices begun by his father Asa. His religious policy was not confined to this negative aspect; he took positive steps to promote religious teaching among the people. In the third year of his reign a high-level team was sent on a tour all over the country, a kind of mobile 'open university' with five royal princes, two priests and nine Levites as its faculty. Their task was to expound 'the book of the Law of the Lord', possibly an early version of the Book of Deuteronomy that was to appear in the reign of Josiah more than two centuries later. The pious monarch liked to move round his realm in person and give encouragement to the observance of the faith.

Jehoshaphat also established a judicial hierarchy. Judges were appointed in all the cities, and the king laid down rules for the conduct of their office. 'Consider what you do, for you judge not for man but for the Lord . . . for there is no perversion of justice with the Lord our God, or partiality, or taking bribes.' (II Chronicles 19:6, 7) In Jerusalem a high court was set up for the whole country, its members drawn from both the religious establishment and distinguished citizens. The high priest Amariah presided over the court 'in all matters of the Lord' (religious issues) and Zebadiah, the chief royal official, 'in all the king's matters' (secular issues). The king enjoined the tribunal to 'deal courageously, may the Lord be with the upright!'

In the Book of Joshua there is a list of the towns in Judah grouped into ten districts. Scholars suggest that this passage reflects an administrative reorganization that took place in the time of Jehoshaphat, with the integrated areas of Benjamin comprising an eleventh district. If so, Jehoshaphat's central control from Jerusalem, exercised through district governors, took the same lines as the system that had been introduced by Solomon for the whole of the United Kingdom.

Jehoshaphat died in the twenty-fifth year of his reign and was succeeded by his son Jehoram (849–842 BC).

7

The House of Omri

In the kingdom of Israel Baasha was succeeded by his son Elah (877–876 BC). Before he had reigned two years this inglorious monarch was murdered while getting drunk in the home of his steward. The assassination was carried out by an officer called Zimri, who was 'commander of half his chariots'. Zimri proclaimed himself king in Tirzah the capital, where he 'reigned' for just one week – long enough for him to kill all the males in the families of his predecessors Baasha and Elah and even of their main supporters. At the time most of the army was again engaged in the siege of Gibbethon (where Baasha had murdered his own royal master), and it was there that the army general Omri was proclaimed king by the field troops. He marched on Tirzah and took it without much resistance. Zimri committed suicide by setting the citadel alight and dying in the flames.

For a year or more the kingdom was torn by civil war between the followers of Omri and those of a rival candidate called Tibni, about whom nothing more than his name is known. The confused struggle ended with Tibni dead and Omri the new king and the undisputed strongman of Israel. During his rule (876–869 BC) and that of his son Ahab (869–850 BC), the kingdom of Israel was to reach a level of importance and achievement it had not known before and would not know again.

Omri was a man of unusual capacity and strength of will. His firm government gave the kingdom a badly needed period of internal stability. He was therefore able to devote himself to external policies, mainly with four neighbouring states, Judah, Phoenicia, Aram-Damascus and Moab.

The half-century of intermittent warfare between the two Israelite kingdoms had come to an end, and the border was stabilized. Omri and Asa, his contemporary in Judah, maintained a peaceful coexistence that later developed into an alliance between their sons, Ahab of Israel and Jehoshaphat of Judah.

Omri renewed the cooperative ties that David and Solomon had enjoyed with Phoenicia on the Mediterranean coast to the west of the kingdom of Israel. The friendship was sealed by the marriage of Omri's crown prince Ahab to Jezebel, the daughter of King Ethbaal of Sidon. As in the days of the United Monarchy, the relationship was of great economic benefit to both sides. The Phoenicians were a nation of traders, with little agricultural hinterland. They could supply Israel with forest products, minerals and manufactured goods, in exchange for the olive oil from the hills of Galilee and Ephraim, and the wheat and other food-stuffs from the fertile fields of the Sharon plain, the Jezreel valley, the Hula and Gilead. The two countries had a common interest in the over-land caravan routes – the Via Maris that came from Egypt and crossed Israel, and the King's Highway that traversed Israel territory in Trans-jordan. Omri extended southward his control over the desert route by reasserting Hebrew domination of the kingdom of Moab, on the table-land east of the Dead Sea. There is a reference to this fact in the famous Mesha Stele, an inscribed basalt tablet found in 1868 by a Prussian missionary at Dibon, the ancient capital of Moab. The stone was erected by Mesha, the durable ninth-century-BC king of Moab in gratitude to his god Chemosh for delivering him from Israelite rule. 'As for Omri, king of Israel', the stele states, 'he humbled Moab many years, for Chemosh was angry with his land.'

A little later the kingdom of Judah became a third partner with Israel and Tyre in the trade routes. As overlord of Edom (the desert kingdom in the Negev and southern Jordan), Judah had access to the sector of the King's Highway below Moab.

With his other frontiers secure, Omri was better able to resist his aggressive Syrian neighbour to the north-east. Under its king, Ben-hadad, Aram-Damascus had subjugated the smaller Aramean king-doms in the area, and had begun to encroach on Israel. Intervening in the brief war between Asa of Judah and Baasha of Israel, Syrian forces had penetrated as far south as the present town of Tiberias on the western shore of the Sea of Galilee. They had not withdrawn altogether, retaining their gains in northern Jordan as far as Ramoth-gilead, a key town on the King's Highway just south of the Yarmuk river. An expansionist Syria posed a direct threat to the Galilee region of Israel and to the whole of Trans-jordan. Omri was able to contain this danger but not to eliminate it, and the struggle with Aram-Damascus would continue in the reign of his son Ahab. The economic penetration of Aram-Damascus was shown by the fact that bazaars owned by Syrian shopkeepers were found in the capital of Israel as mentioned in the Bible.

In the sixth year of his reign, Omri launched the major project of his reign, the building of a new capital at a place that would be called Samaria, ten kilometres north-west of Shechem. The site was a conspicuous hill commanding both the road northward from Shechem to the valley of Jezreel, and a lateral road from the Jordan valley to the coast. From its summit the Mediterranean can be seen thirty-seven kilometres away. The hill was bought from a certain Shemer for two talents of silver. The name of Samaria (Hebrew *Shomron*) may have been derived either from him or from the Hebrew word for a watchtower.

Conscious of the prestige of Jerusalem Omri wanted a national centre for his kingdom more impressive than the undistinguished town of Tirzah, to which Jeroboam had moved from Shechem. As a former general Omri was also attracted by the natural defences of this freestanding hill, very steep on three sides, and with its summit ninety metres above the surrounding flat fields.

The summit was levelled down to bedrock as a site for a rectangular citadel containing the palace complex. It was protected by a wall of square stone blocks laid with great skill: the lower courses of some sections are still intact, two thousand eight hundred years later. On the more gradual southern slope below this acropolis lay the city, also enclosed by a massive stone wall dating from the reign of Ahab or a little later. Isaiah referred to Samaria as 'the proud crown of Ephraim on the head of a rich valley'. In course of time the whole of the surrounding hill-region became known as Samaria and its inhabitants as Samaritans.

Samaria was destroyed by the Assyrian army in 722 BC and rebuilt seven centuries later by Herod the Great. He called it Sebaste, from the Greek name of his patron, the Emperor Augustus, and placed a splendid temple on the summit where the citadel of Omri and Ahab had stood.

Omri is given curt treatment in the Bible, which states that he 'did what was evil in the sight of the Lord, and did more evil than all who were before him'. (I Kings 16:25) This disfavour may be attributed to his special relationship with the Phoenicians and the marriage he arranged between his son Ahab and the Sidonite princess Jezebel, which opened the door to pagan influences. But there is no doubt that he gained a new regional importance for the kingdom of Israel. A century later it was still referred to in Assyrian records as 'Bit Humri', The House of Omri.

AHAB

Under Ahab (869–850 BC) Israel reached the zenith of its strength and affluence. He developed the external policies of his father: good relations with Judah, economic cooperation with the Phoenician city-states, and containment of Aram-Damascus. He continued the building and fortification of the new capital at Samaria and carried out extensive construction projects elsewhere in the country. Living standards rose, but the gap between rich and poor widened. In the latter part of his reign Ahab ran into increasing religious and social problems, that were to wreck the dynasty after his death. In the Bible he is roundly condemned for religious laxity in terms similar to those used about his father Omri. In the scriptural account of his reign, the forces of light and darkness that swirled about Ahab are personified by the prophet Elijah and Queen Jezebel.

THE SYRIAN WARS

In the chronic war with Aram-Damascus during Ahab's reign three campaigns are recounted in the Bible. The literal account of the first one has Ben-hadad with thirty-two of his vassal kings laying siege to Samaria. He sent arrogant messages demanding that Ahab surrender all his treasure of gold and silver, together with 'your fairest wives and children', otherwise the Syrian troops would be sent in to seize them, and the city would be reduced to dust. Ahab flung back the classic saying 'let not him that gird on his armour boast himself as he that puts it off'. The reply reached Ben-hadad while he and his comrades were drinking at their ease in their *succot* (pavilions). He ordered his troops to advance on Samaria but they were routed in a surprise counterattack launched by Ahab in the heat of the midday sun. In his *The Art of Warfare in Biblical Lands* Professor Yigael Yadin of the Hebrew University of Jerusalem reconstructs this battle in a different way. When it is said that Ben-hadad was drinking in *succot*, Professor Yadin reads that word not as 'pavilions' but as the town of Succot east of the Jordan river.

From here the Syrian forces would have advanced across the river at the ford of Adamah (today the Damiya bridge) and up the Wadi Fara, which closes into a narrow defile near the top. Squeezing through it, the chariot forces of Ben-hadad would have been very vulnerable to attack. (In September 1918, during the Palestine campaign in the First World War, a Turkish army winding its way down from Nablus was decimated by British planes in this same defile of Wadi Fara.)

Ben-hadad's military advisers pointed out to him the two lessons to be learnt from his defeat. The first concerned military topography – the dangers of attacking a mountain people in their own terrain. 'Their gods are gods of the hills, and so they were stronger than we; but let us fight against them in the plain, and surely we shall be stronger than they.' (I Kings 20:23) It was the story over again of the Philistine chariots fighting against the Israelite highlanders in previous centuries. The second lesson concerned command. The conduct of battles, they maintained, should be left to the professional soldiers, and not to civilian amateurs like Ben-hadad's bibulous vassal kings: 'And do this: remove the kings, each from his post, and put commanders in their places'. (I Kings 20:24)

By the following spring Ben-hadad had mustered and equipped a fresh army 'horse for horse and chariot for chariot'. Apparently he intended to advance into Israel by a more northerly route, round the lower end of the Sea of Galilee and along the Jezreel valley, so as to give battle on level ground. Ahab anticipated this move and intercepted the Syrian force in the hills east of the Sea of Galilee, between the gorge of the Yarmuk river and the city of Aphek. After they had faced one another for seven days, the battle was joined, and the hemmed-in Syrian army heavily defeated. Ben-hadad himself escaped into Aphek and handed himself over when that city fell to the Israelites. He was released on an understanding that he would hand back Israelite towns and territory that had been taken and occupied by his father, and also grant to Israelite traders the same special privileges in the bazaars of Damascus as the Syrians had previously enjoyed in Samaria.

For the next three years there was a truce between Israel and Aram-Damascus. The background was the rising Assyrian threat to both countries. Five centuries had gone by since the Hittite empire to the north of Canaan had disintegrated and Egyptian power to the south had declined. During this period Israelites, Canaanites, Arameans and Philistines had played out their parts on the local stage. They had made wars, alliances and trading ventures between themselves outside the orbit of any Great Power. In the ninth century BC this regional seclusion ended. Assyria had become the dominant power in the Mesopotamian basin and started to push westwards towards the Mediterranean. Some of its might and splendour is conveyed in Lord Byron's poem 'The Destruction of Sennacherib', the opening words of which read:

> The Assyrians came down like a wolf on the fold,
> Their cohorts were gleaming in purple and gold.

For the next few centuries the shadow of Nineveh, the capital of the Assyrian empire, would lie across the Near East.

With their arrogant bearded faces, their winged-bull effigies, their obsession with war and their cruel treatment of conquered nations, the Assyrians were the 'herrenfolk' of the ancient Near East. They built up the most powerful military machine known to man till then. Among the treasures in the British Museum are reliefs from the palace walls of Assyrian kings, and the huge bronze gates of one of them. They depict the military campaigns in superb detail: the spearsmen, archers and slingmen of the infantry; the cavalry armed with lance or bow; the powerful chariot squadrons; the battering rams, mobile towers, scaling ladders and tunnelling sappers in action against fortified cities; the dejected lines of captives and the piles of dismembered corpses.

In the first half of the 9th century BC, during Omri's reign, the army of Asshur-nasir-pal II had reached northern Syria and the Phoenician city-states on the coast, exacted heavy tribute from them and withdrawn. In 853 BC, the Assyrian army again set out westward from Nineveh, now under Asshur-nasir-pal's son and successor, Shalmanezer III. Alarm spread through the region. Ahab of Israel and Ben-hadad of Aram-Damascus were prominent in a coalition of local kingdoms formed to stop the Assyrian advance. The confrontation took place at Karkar on the Orontes river in northern Syria. In an inscription on his palace wall Shalmanezer boasted of victory over the combined forces of eleven (possibly twelve) kings. 'They came up against me for a decisive battle. I smote fourteen thousand men of their armies with the sword . . . And I crossed the Orontes over their bodies before there was a bridge over it . . .' In the list of kings and the forces contributed by each of them, the inscription credits 'Ahab the Israelite' with having furnished 'two thousand chariots, as many as all other allies combined, and ten thousand infantry'. It is possible that this huge Israelite chariot force

94

included squadrons provided by king Jehoshaphat of Judah, though he is not specifically mentioned among the kings listed. In spite of Shalmanezer's claims, the battle must have been indecisive, since the Assyrian forces withdrew and did not reappear for another five years.

Like other rich and energetic rulers, including Solomon before him and Herod the Great after him, Ahab gave his era tangible expression in an ambitious building programme.

He developed the handsome new capital at Samaria founded by his father Omri, and strengthened its fortifications, adding a city wall thick enough to resist battering rams. The 'ivory house' he built marked both the affluence of his court and the influence of Queen Jezebel's Phoenician culture. In the excavations at Samaria hundreds of carved pieces of ivory were found, mostly used as inlay for furniture. Ivory was regarded at that time as a rare and beautiful substance with a value shared only with gold, precious stones and spices.

Outside the capital Ahab's main construction projects were at Hazor and Megiddo, two of Solomon's three 'chariot cities'. At Hazor the archaeological remains show that Solomon's city was largely destroyed by fire. In Ahab's reconstruction, most of the western half of the mound was covered by a large, strongly built citadel, with two parallel halls flanked by smaller rooms on three sides. The entrance was marked by handsome columns with ornamental capitals and a huge lintel. The space that had been taken up by Solomon's buildings was extended eastward to include the whole of the twelve-hectare mound, enclosed by thick stone walls.

The destruction of Megiddo at the edge of the valley of Jezreel can be attributed to the Pharaoh Shishak, whose campaign through Judah and Israel took place five years after Solomon's death. Here, too, the citadel and public buildings were rebuilt by Ahab, with fortifications similar to those at Hazor. The excavations on this site revealed the ruins of extensive stables. They comprised five long buildings, each with two parallel rows of eleven stalls, containing stone pillars, to which the horses were tethered, and limestone mangers. Altogether there was accommodation for 492 animals. It was accepted until recently that these were stables built by Solomon for his chariot horses, and were therefore popularly referred to as 'Solomon's stables'. The puzzling feature about this supposition was that the city walls on the same level were of a type introduced after Solomon's reign. The characteristic

Solomonic fortifications used the casemate wall, a double wall enclosing small rooms. In Ahab's time the casemate wall was abandoned because it was unable to withstand the Assyrian battering ram, a potent siege weapon. Instead Ahab's military engineers adopted thick walls of solid stone blocks, containing salients and recesses. This type of ninth-century city wall was found at Megiddo. In 1961 Yadin showed that *below* it were the remains of Solomon's casemate wall. His conclusion was that Ahab and not Solomon had built the stables, though using blocks of stone lying on the site from Solomon's buildings.

Ahab's engineers are thought to have been responsible also for the large-scale and complex water systems at Megiddo and Hazor. An assured water supply for a walled city was the key to its survival under siege, in a country where summers are long and hot, rainfall is confined to the winter and early spring, and there are periodic droughts. Water stored in cisterns provided an inadequate supply for a long siege. Towns were located near natural springs, but as a rule the towns were built on hill-tops for defence while the springs were in low ground outside the walls. The blocking of the water sources by an enemy could in itself force a city to surrender, as happened when Joab was besieging Rab-both-ammon in David's reign. One logical but difficult solution was to sink a deep shaft within the walls, and on reaching the water level to drive a tunnel through to the spring. One example is at the 'pool of Gibeon' where a battle took place between the opposing Israelite forces led by Joab and Abner.

This solution was applied at Megiddo. The water system consists of a shaft twenty-four metres deep, with stairs leading to a horizontal tunnel sixty-eight metres long that ends in a spring in the lower slope of the hill. Acting on the Megiddo precedent Yadin found a similar though larger system at Hazor, also dating from Ahab's period. The shaft is forty metres deep, with a stairway cut into the rock walls leading down to the entrance of a tunnel which ends at an outside spring. A century and a half after Ahab, King Hezekiah ensured Jerusalem's water supply by a tunnel connecting the Gihon spring outside the wall with the pool of Siloam within.

From the time of Solomon the advanced Phoenicians had had a far-reaching impact on Israelite life. In some spheres – commerce, naviga-tion, architecture and the arts – the Hebrew nation had learnt much from these versatile neighbours. The negative aspect was the encroachment of Phoenician deities and cults on the austere monotheism the Israelite tribes had brought out of the desert. In the ninth-century-BC kingdom of Israel this process was increased by its close ties with Tyre and Sidon, and the substantial, half-assimilated Canaanite elements in the local population.

The struggle of the Mosaic faith against these pagan influences was brought to a head by the missionary zeal of Ahab's Phoenician wife Jezebel. She was determined to convert her adopted land to the worship of Melkart the Phoenician god 'Baal' and Ashtaroth (Astarte), the goddess of fertility. Four hundred and fifty priests or 'prophets' of Baal were maintained by Jezebel in the capital. Shrines to her native gods sprang up on the hill-tops, and a temple to Baal was constructed in the palace grounds. The Israelite priests who resisted these inroads were eliminated or driven into hiding. These imported practices, like Phoenician styles in dress, furniture and ornaments, became the fashion among the upper classes and the wealthy merchants, though the rural peasantry was less affected by them and clung to the ancestral faith. (This pattern was to repeat itself in the struggle against Greek ways in the Hellenist period centuries later.)

It is hard to fathom why Ahab should have tolerated the pagan trends. To some extent he must have been dominated by his strong-willed and aristocratic consort. It is also likely that he was immersed in practical affairs of State – the wars with Aram-Damascus, building projects and day-to-day administration – and left to his wife the religious interests that mattered a great deal more to her than they did to him. His lack of religious involvement was illustrated at the outset of his last war against the Syrians. It was not he but his God-fearing ally, Jehoshaphat king of Judah, who called for divine guidance and blessing for the campaign.

ELIJAH THE TISHBITE

The backlash against Jezebel and her pagan gods focused on the gaunt and terrifying figure of the prophet Elijah the Tishbite. Emerging from an unknown background in Gilead, across the Jordan, and clad in the hairshirt and loincloth of the ascetic, Elijah erupts with dramatic force into the Biblical narrative, about half-way through Ahab's reign. He suddenly appeared before the king and predicted a grim drought: 'As the

Lord the God of Israel lives, before whom I stand, there shall be neither dew nor rain these years . . .' (I Kings 17:1) These words asserted the Lord's control over the forces of nature as against the Phoenician Baal, who was a rain-god. Before the astounded Ahab could deal with the wild-looking man of God, Elijah had vanished again. He crossed the Jordan and sat as a recluse at 'the brook Cherith', a desolate spot on the Trans-jordan plateau, where he was miraculously fed by ravens. When the water in the stream dried up, Elijah sought refuge across the Phoenician border in a town near the great port city of Sidon. He lived in the upstairs room of a poor widow's home and performed wonders for her, resuscitating her child who had died, and keeping the three of them alive on her tiny stock of flour and olive oil that constantly replenished itself. (Similar miracles would later be attributed to Jesus of Nazareth.)

Nearly three years after his first meeting with Ahab, Elijah was told by the Lord that the drought would break soon, and that he should seek out the king again. The prophet set out on foot to Samaria, and on the way met Obadiah, the royal steward. He had been sent out by the king to search for grazing, to 'go through the land to all the springs of water and to all the valleys; perhaps we may find grass and save the horses and mules alive, and not lose some of the animals'. (I Kings 18:5) The official was a pious man who had courageously hidden a number of prophets in a cave and fed them to save them from Jezebel's persecution. He treated Elijah with the deference due to a holy man, and warned him that the king had hunted everywhere for him. The steward was reluctant to risk his life by telling the king that Elijah wanted to see him.

However on Elijah's insistence the message was delivered. Ahab hurried out to meet him, and called out: 'Is it you, you troubler of Israel?' The totally undismayed prophet flung back: 'I have not troubled Israel; but you have, and your father's house, because you have forsaken the commandments of the Lord and followed the Baals.' (I Kings 18:18) He then made the imperious demand that the king call an assembly for him on Mount Carmel, to be attended by all the pagan prophets maintained by Jezebel. Strangely enough the king complied. He must have been awed by the complete authority with which this unkempt man of God addressed him, and hoped that the prophet who had predicted the drought and famine would find a way to end them.

The trial of strength that followed on Mount Carmel was a climactic moment in this long conflict between monotheism and paganism. In the presence of King Ahab Elijah stood before the crowd and called out:

'How long will you go limping with two different opinions? If the Lord is God, follow him; but if Baal, then follow him.' (I Kings 18:21) He threw out a challenge to the prophets of Baal. Let each side cut up a bullock, lay the pieces on a heap of firewood, and call out to his deity to see which one would send down fire to consume the sacrifice. The first to start were the pagan priests. All day they leapt round their altar, cried out to Baal and slashed themselves with knives in their frenzy. But nothing happened. Elijah taunted them: 'Cry aloud, for he is a god; either he is musing, or he has gone aside, or he is on a journey, or perhaps he is asleep and must be awakened.' (I Kings 18:27) Again nothing happened.

It was now Elijah's turn. Towards sunset he rebuilt a ruined altar with twelve stones, one for each of the tribes. He stacked the firewood, laid the pieces of meat on it and dug a trench round it. To make the test more convincing, the altar was drenched with water. When all was ready, Elijah called out to the Lord. At once fire came down on to the altar and set the wood alight, consuming the sacrifice. The crowd fell on their faces in awe, shouting: 'The Lord, he is God: the Lord he is God.' (I Kings 18:39) In this atmosphere of tension and triumph the pagan priests were seized and dragged to the small Kishon river, where they were killed.

The exhausted Elijah rested, sitting on the ground with his head between his knees, while his servant was repeatedly sent to the top of the ridge to see whether the rain was approaching. The seventh time, the servant reported: 'behold a little cloud like a man's hand is rising out of the sea'. Soon the storm was upon them, and the drought was broken by a torrential downpour. With the exultant prophet loping ahead, his cloak tucked up round his waist, the king set out for home in his chariot. Arriving back at his winter palace at Jezreel, twenty-seven kilometres down the valley from Mount Carmel, Ahab had to break the bad news of the death of her pagan priests to his formidable queen. In a fury she sought Elijah's blood in revenge, but the prophet had vanished again.

This time Elijah headed southward to Beersheba. Once more lonely and exiled, and oppressed by a sense of failure, he set off on a solitary trek across the desert to Mount Sinai, to renew himself at the fount of his faith. Here he had a personal revelation, hearing the 'still, small voice' of God, who charged him to resume his mission. On his way northward through the Jordan valley Elijah saw a youth ploughing

99

with a team of oxen. His name was Elisha. The prophet threw his mantle over the young man, and from then on he remained Elijah's faithful companion and disciple.

The prophet's final encounter with Ahab arose out of the incident with Naboth's vineyard. It adjoined the grounds of the winter palace at Jezreel, and Ahab was eager to acquire it as a vegetable garden. Naboth declined to sell it or exchange it for a better vineyard elsewhere, on the legitimate ground that it was ancestral family property. This refusal left Ahab 'vexed and sullen'. When Jezebel heard the reason for his black mood, she scorned the very notion that the king should be balked by the legal rights of one of his subjects. She decided to settle matters in her own way. She arranged for false letters to be sent in the king's name and over his seal to the local authorities in the town of Jezreel. They were to find two unscrupulous men who would bring charges against Naboth of uttering blasphemy against God and treason against the king; and he was to be condemned and stoned to death. This judicial frame-up, ostensibly on the king's orders, was duly carried out. By law the property of a convicted rebel automatically became vested in the ruler. On learning what had happened, Ahab immediately travelled from Samaria to Jezreel to take possession of the coveted vineyard.

The proceedings illustrate that a Hebrew king was not above the law, and could not simply expropriate property that he wanted. That is why Jezebel had to devise a devious stratagem that outwardly seemed to comply with due process of law. The legal niceties may have been satisfied, but not the social conscience of the community, with Elijah as its spokesman.

The prophet descended once more on the king and thundered at him: 'Have you killed, and also taken possession? . . . In the place where dogs licked up the blood of Naboth shall dogs lick your own blood.' (I Kings 21:19) Ahab's whole dynasty, Elijah predicted, would be destroyed.

The king did not attempt to defend himself. Muttering dejectedly to the fierce old prophet 'have you found me, O my enemy?' he dressed in sackcloth and fasted as a mark of repentance.

AHAB'S LAST CAMPAIGN

With the ebbing of the immediate danger after the battle of Karkar, the anti-Assyrian coalition fell apart, and its members reverted to their previous feuds. War broke out once more between Israel and Aram-

Damascus, which had reneged on the commitment to evacuate occupied Israelite territory, and still held the northern part of Transjordan down to and including Ramoth-gilead.

The improved relations between Samaria and Jerusalem made possible a military alliance against Damascus. Jehoshaphat came on a royal visit to the northern capital, the first of its kind in the history of the two kingdoms, and was given a sumptuous welcome by Ahab. The visitor was urged to join in an operation to recapture Ramoth-gilead and he was willing to do so provided guidance was first sought from the Lord. For this purpose four hundred prophets were summoned by Ahab to an assembly in front of the city gate, where the two monarchs sat on thrones, wearing shining armour. Ahab put the question to the prophets 'Shall we go to battle against Ramoth-gilead, or shall I forbear?' to which they all gave an affirmative answer. The leading prophet, Zedekiah, underlined the message with a tangible metaphor. He produced a pair of iron horns with which the Arameans would be gored to death. Jehoshaphat was not entirely convinced by this chorus of prophetic yes-men. He asked Ahab whether there was any other local prophet who had not been drawn into consultation. Yes, Ahab replied, there was one called Micaiah, 'but I hate him, for he never prophesies good concerning me, but always evil'. To satisfy his devout ally Ahab sent a messenger to fetch Micaiah. The prophet was warned by the messenger that he had better fall into line with the others, which he did. This was so out of character that the king brushed aside his positive prediction and ordered him to come out with his true opinion. This time the dour man of God did not mince his words. He foretold defeat for the Israelite forces and death for the king. The Lord, he said, had sent an evil spirit to tell lies through the mouths of the other prophets gathered there, and so entice the king to his fate. The two monarchs were not swayed by this lone dissenting voice. Ahab ordered that Micaiah be arrested and kept on bread and water until his own safe return.

All the same Ahab must have been disturbed by Micaiah's words. When the battle was joined at Ramoth-gilead he took the unusual precaution of disguising himself. Ben-hadad had instructed his commanders to concentrate the attack on the person of the king of Israel. At first they mistook Jehoshaphat for their target, until they heard his battle cry. In spite of his disguise Ahab was fatally wounded by a Syrian archer 'who drew his bow at a venture'. The king's chariot driver drew him out of the thick of the battle, and with great gallantry Ahab propped himself up in his chariot facing the enemy, to sustain the morale of his men. He died at sunset. The Israelite forces withdrew in defeat, and Jehoshaphat returned to Jerusalem.

The hostility of the biblical writers followed Ahab to the grave. To the mention of his funeral in Samaria there is a stinging footnote: 'And they washed the chariot by the pool of Samaria, and the dogs licked up his blood, and the harlots washed themselves in it, according to the word of the Lord which he had spoken. ' (I Kings 22:38)

8

Decades of Decline

After the death of Ahab in 850 BC and that of Jehoshaphat of Judah in 849 BC both kingdoms entered a period of weakness and decline that lasted more than sixty years. Their fortunes would revive in the eighth century during the long and successful reigns of Jeroboam II in Israel and Uzziah in Judah.

Ahab was followed on the throne by his eldest son Ahaziah, whose mother was Jezebel. His brief and inglorious two-year reign (850–849 BC) was marked by another round of trouble with his father's redoubtable adversary, the prophet Elijah. Ahaziah had badly injured himself by falling through the lattice window of an upper chamber in the palace of Samaria. He sent messengers to inquire of 'Baal-zebub, the god of Ekron' whether he would recover. (Baal-zebub means 'god of the flies' and is a derisive corruption of the name Baal-zebul, 'god of the lofty place'. Spelt Beelzebub, he figures in the New Testament as a name for Satan.) The messengers were intercepted by Elijah. He scornfully told them to return and ask their royal master whether he did not know that there was a God in Israel? Ahaziah, added the prophet, would die without getting up again from his sickbed. The angry king sent an officer with fifty men to seize the prophet, but they were miraculously killed by fire from heaven. A second company was wiped out in the same way. The captain of the third company threw himself on the mercy of Elijah, who went back with the soldiers to the palace and repeated his prediction to Ahaziah. The latter died soon after.

Ahaziah is also mentioned in connection with the ill-fated attempt by King Jehoshaphat of Judah to revive the sea route to the Red Sea from the southern port of Ezion-geber. According to Chronicles, Judah and Israel were partners in this enterprise, but the ships were wrecked because of divine disapproval of Ahaziah. The Book of Kings says merely that Ahaziah wanted his sailors to be included in the ships' crews but was rebuffed by Jehoshaphat.

As Ahaziah left no son the throne went to his younger brother Jehoram (849–842 BC). He is not to be confused with his contemporary in Judah, Jehoram the son of Jehoshaphat, who was connected to the Omri dynasty by his marriage to Athaliah.

In the negative scale applied by the Bible to the House of Omri, Jehoram is treated a little less severely than his father Ahab and his grandfather Omri. It is mentioned to his credit that he took down a 'pillar of Baal' erected by Ahab.

THE CAMPAIGN AGAINST MOAB

Mesha the king of Moab had been subdued by Omri, and became a tribute-paying vassal of the kingdom of Israel. The annual payment in kind from his pastoral people comprised 'a hundred thousand lambs, and the wool of a hundred rams'. It is likely that Mesha threw off the yoke of Israel and regained his independence late in the reign of Ahab, while the latter was fully committed to the war with Aram-Damascus. With the Israelite defeat at Ramoth-gilead, the death of Ahab and the accession of the ineffectual Ahaziah, Mesha pushed northward into Israelite territory and captured several towns. At one of them, according to Mesha's commemorative stele, seven thousand Israelites were slaughtered.

On succeeding his brother Ahaziah to the throne of Israel Jehoram decided to launch a campaign against Moab, and he proposed to Jehoshaphat of Judah that they should join forces. Jehoshaphat answered without reservation that 'I will go; I am as you are, my people as your people, my horses as your horses'. (II Kings 3:7) The cooperation of Judah was essential to Jehoram's plan of campaign, based on a line of advance through the 'wilderness of Edom' round the lower end of the Dead Sea, to invade Moab from the south. He calculated that this would be the Moabite 'soft underbelly', since Mesha had concentrated on fortifying his northern frontier. The Israelite forces were joined by the king of Edom, a vassal of Judah.

After seven days of marching through broken desert terrain, they found themselves up against a very potent enemy: thirst. The water supply carried with them had run out for men and beast alike. Again, it was the devout Jehoshaphat who suggested that they find a prophet

The valley of Jezreel. Control of key towns
in this valley was of vital strategic importance to the Philistines
in their battle against the Israelites under Saul's command.

ABOVE A scene from the Battle of Mount Gilboa where Saul fell upon his own sword.

LEFT Samuel, called to appear before Saul by the witch of Endor, prophesied the defeat of the Israelites.

Renowned for his wisdom, Solomon is here portrayed making his celebrated decision concerning the motherhood of a child.

Samaria was the last stronghold of the Northern Kingdom of Israel; its capture by the Assyrians in 722 BC ended that kingdom.

King Rehoboam planned to reunite Israel by force but was dissuaded by the prophet Shemaiah.

The Temple of Amon-Ra, built by Pharaoh Shishak across the sacred lake, Karnak. Names of the towns which Shishak's forces occupied during their invasion of Israel and Judah are inscribed on the wall.

LEFT An aura of mystery surrounds Elijah, one of the most memorable of the Hebrew prophets. He first appeared before King Ahab to predict a drought: nothing is known of him before this and he is said to have finally vanished up to heaven in a blazing chariot.

ABOVE Elijah, Ahab and Jezebel in Naboth's vineyard – this was to be Ahab's final encounter with the prophet.

LEFT Athaliah was the only female monarch of either of the Hebrew kingdoms. This eighth-century BC ivory artifact from Nimrod depicts a woman seated on a throne.

OPPOSITE The Black Obelisk of Shalmaneser III. This detail shows Jehu, son of Omri, kneeling before the Assyrian king and is the the only known contemporary portrait of an Israelite monarch.

BELOW Excavation at Hazor has yielded this Israelite storehouse with columns and casemate walls dating from the tenth century BC, the time of Omri.

RIGHT Isaiah, the greatest of the Hebrew prophets.

BELOW The inscription from Hezekiah's tunnel; written in classical Hebrew it records Hezekiah's steps to ensure a water supply for Jerusalem in time of siege.

One of the stone wall reliefs from Sennacherib's palace at Nineveh. Dating from the seventh century BC, the cuneiform inscription reads: 'Sennacherib, King of Assyria, sitting on his throne while the spoil from the city of Lachish passed before him.'

The siege of Jerusalem by Nebuchadnezzar.

The prophet Jeremiah continually warned of the fall
of Jerusalem, despite the fact that the Babylonian troops had withdrawn
and it was generally believed that a reprieve was at hand.

to invoke the help of the Lord. One of the officers knew where to find the wonder-working Elisha, and all three kings went to visit him. The prophet made clear that he would have no dealings with the king of Israel, the country where his beloved master Elijah had been persecuted. He was willing to be helpful but only for the sake of Jehoshaphat. Elisha called for a minstrel, and under the influence of the music, 'the power of the Lord came upon him'. Pointing to a dry watercourse he predicted that 'you shall not see wind or rain but that stream-bed shall be filled with water . . .' (II Kings 3:17) Early next morning water came swirling down from the hills, in what was apparently one of the flash floods not uncommon in the desert. Filled with the red sandstone dust that gave Edom its name ('red' in Hebrew), the water looked like blood in the glint of the dawn light. The Moabites watching from a distance thought the invaders had started slaying one another, and rushed in to collect the booty. They were repulsed with heavy losses.

The expeditionary force crossed the undefended frontier and advanced into the heart of Moab. Urged on by Elisha, they adopted a scorched-earth policy. 'And they overthrew the cities, and on every good piece of land every man threw a stone, until it was covered; they stopped every spring of water, and felled all the good trees . . .' (II Kings 3:25) The old capital, Kir-hareseth, was surrounded and taken. The king of Moab tried to stop the advance by throwing a counter-attack against the Edomite auxiliary units, but it failed. As a last resort Mesha took the desperate and dramatic step of sacrificing his eldest son to the national god, Chemosh. The result is tersely stated: 'And there came great wrath upon Israel; and they withdrew from him and returned to their own land.' (II Kings 3:27) The question remains, why should the Israelites have abandoned their campaign so abruptly, with victory and the conquest of Moab almost within their grasp? Presumably, since the human burnt-offering had been made on the city wall in their sight, they were filled with horror and superstitious dread of the foreign god who had been so grimly prodded to protect his realm.

The war between Israel and Aram-Damascus also flared up again in the reign of Jehoram. A Syrian army under King Ben-hadad II laid siege to Samaria, and there was a real danger that the city would be starved into surrender. The little food left in it changed hands at exorbitant black-market prices – for instance, the head of an ass for eighty shekels of silver, and a cupful of dove's dung for five shekels. Walking along the city walls one day, King Jehoram heard two women quarrelling, and he stopped to ask them what was wrong. One of them explained that, left with nothing to eat they had made a pact to boil and share their infants in turn. Hers had been consumed, but the other woman had hidden her child and refused to produce it. Sick at heart the king tore his clothes, and passers-by noted that he wore sackcloth next to his skin. His anguish turned to anger against the prophet Elisha, who had counselled resistance in the name of the Lord. Bursting into Elisha's house the king cried out rebelliously: 'This trouble is from the Lord! Why should I wait for the Lord any longer?' (II Kings 6:33) Elisha solemnly promised that by the following day there would be cheap and abundant supplies for everyone. When a royal officer with the king expressed scepticism, Elisha lashed out at him that he would not be about to eat the food.

At their habitual place outside the city gate sat four lepers shunned by their fellowmen. Weak from hunger they decided at dusk to approach the Syrian camp in the hope of scavenging scraps to eat. To their astonishment the camp was deserted. Noises at night had been interpreted by the Syrians as the sound of troops coming in to raise the siege, and they had fled in fear of being cut off. The lepers stuffed themselves with food, found and hid some valuables and then realized they would be in trouble if they did not get word back to the city. They therefore returned and told the sentries at the gate what they had seen. At first the king feared this was a Syrian ruse to lure the defenders into the open. He was persuaded to send out a reconnaissance patrol of two men mounted on the last of the surviving horses. They followed the trail of the Syrians to the ford across the Jordan, and came back to report that the siege was indeed over. The gates were flung open and the frenzied crowd rushed out to reach the Syrian supplies. The officer whose disbelief had so irked Elisha was knocked over and trampled to death.

JUDAH UNDER JEHOSHAPHAT

Under Jehoshaphat's son and successor Jehoram (849–842 BC), the kingdom of Judah took a sharp plunge downward.

The vassal kingdom of Edom in the south revolted, and when Jehoram sallied out to restore order, his force was surrounded and routed. One consequence of this setback was the loss of access through the Negev to the port of Ezion-geber, the gateway to the Red Sea. There was also some trouble from Philistia, and the former Canaanite city of Libnah in the Judean foothills was lost. Inside the kingdom there was a slackening of the religious fibre, attributed largely to the influence of Jehoram's queen, Athaliah, a princess of the Omri dynasty in the northern kingdom.

The Book of Chronicles makes much of the connection with this abhorred dynasty, and of Jehoram's wickedness. It is alleged that he murdered his younger brothers when he mounted the throne and that he permitted pagan practices. The Chronicler adds that he was punished with a fatal disease of the bowels, predicted in a prophetic letter from Elijah; and that when he died in agony, 'His people made no fire in his honour ... and he departed with no one's regret.' (II Chronicles 21:19, 20) He was succeeded by his son Ahaziah, whose reign lasted less than a year (842 BC).

Ahaziah joined Jehoram, king of Israel, in the renewed war with Aram-Damascus, now ruled by Hazael. Once more the fighting raged over possession of Ramoth-gilead, the strategic town east of the Jordan. When King Jehoram was wounded in battle, he handed over command to his general Jehu, and retired to recuperate at his winter palace in Jezreel. Here his ally from Judah, Ahaziah, came to visit him.

The prophet Elisha now instigated a plot to overthrow Jehoram and liquidate the Omri dynasty. He sent a young member of a band of prophets to Ramoth-gilead on a mission to Jehu, who came out of a staff conference to receive the odd visitor. The general was taken aback when the young prophet anointed him king from a flask of holy oil provided by Elisha, and urged him in the Lord's name to wipe out the entire house of Ahab. Returning to the meeting, Jehu related what had happened with the 'mad fellow' who had come to see him. His brother officers took the matter seriously; they leapt to their feet and acclaimed him their king.

With a troop of cavalry behind him, Jehu covered at great speed the eighty kilometres from Gilead across the Jordan valley and up to Jezreel. A watchman reported to Jehoram that he had seen a party approaching in a cloud of dust 'and the driving is like the driving of Jehu the son of Nimshi; for he drives furiously'. (II Kings 9:20) The two kings went out in their chariots to meet him, no doubt anxious to hear what important tidings he brought in such haste. Jehoram called out: 'Is it peace, Jehu?' The crude answer came back: 'What peace can there be, so long as the harlotries and the sorceries of your mother Jezebel are so many?' (II Kings 9:22)

Realizing that they faced treachery, the kings spun their chariots round and made a dash for safety. Jehu drew his bow and loosed an arrow that pierced Jehoram between the shoulder blades, killing him on the spot. Close by was Naboth's vineyard, where some years earlier, when Jehu was in Ahab's bodyguard, he had heard Elijah prophesy a bloody end to the royal house. Jehoram's corpse was now flung into the vineyard. The unfortunate King Ahaziah was also chased and wounded. He managed to reach Megiddo, where he died, and his body was taken to Jerusalem for burial.

The next target was the queen-mother Jezebel, who met her end with the defiant pride of the born aristocrat. As Jehu approached her quarters, she took her stand at an upper window, her face and eyes fastidiously made up and her hair groomed. With biting scorn she called out: 'Is it peace, you Zimri, murderer of your master?' (II Kings 9:31). (Zimri was the army officer who forty years earlier had killed the king and seized power, just as Jehu had now done.) Jehu did not bother to reply. He shouted to her attendants to hurl her down from the window. They did so and 'some of her blood spattered on the wall and on the horses, and they trampled on her'. (II Kings 9:33) Unperturbed, Jehu went into the palace to have a meal. He sent servants out to bury Jezebel, saying with a shrug she was after all a king's daughter. All they found left of her was the skull, hands and feet, for the dogs had eaten the rest. Elijah's savage prediction was thus fulfilled.

The hatred that religious circles felt for Jezebel comes through in the account of her gruesome death. In biblical tradition she remains the symbol of pagan depravity.

There followed a blood-bath of unparalleled scale and ferocity. All the royal entourage in Jezreel was wiped out. Written instructions were sent to the authorities in Samaria to send Jehu the heads of Ahab's descendants, who numbered seventy. The word 'heads' was ambiguous, as it may have meant 'leaders'. The terrified notables in Samaria took the orders literally, killed all the descendants and sent their severed heads to Jezreel in baskets. Jehu exploited the public horror caused by this deed. He ordered the heads to be placed in two heaps at the city gates, where he appeared and said to the crowd: 'You are innocent. It was I who conspired against my master, and slew him; but who struck down all these?' (II Kings 10:9) Jehu then set out for Samaria, encountering on the way and killing a hapless delegation of forty-two persons from Judah. In Samaria Jehu was proclaimed king (842–815 BC). All who were connected with the royal house, or known to be its supporters, were rounded up and executed.

Against the adherents of the Phoenician Baal, Jehu resorted to stratagem. He gave out that he wished personally to offer sacrifices in the temple of Baal in Samaria, and ordered that the priests and followers of the cult from all over the kingdom had to attend, on penalty of death. After he had gone through the motions of making the sacrifice in the packed temple, a company of his troops burst in and slew the whole congregation. The 'pillar of Baal' was then smashed. The building was razed to the ground, and a latrine erected on the site. This concluded the great purge that put an end to the house of Omri and, for the time being, stamped out the pagan cult fostered by Jezebel.

THE JEHU ERA

Jehu's coup represented something more than the seizure of the throne by a ruthless general. It had popular support, for it gave vent to the discontent pent up beneath the power and wealth of the Omri–Ahab period. Behind Jehu were the priests and prophets harried by Jezebel, the peasant farmers racked by drought and taxes, and the soldiers bogged down on the Syrian front far from home.

Jehu soon found that it was easier to destroy a regime than to restore a country. The dynasty that he started was the longest in the history of the northern kingdom, lasting for almost a century; but for most of that time, Jehu and his successors would preside over weakness and decline.

Jehu's accession brought about the collapse of the external policies so carefully fostered by Omri and Ahab. The ties of friendship with the Phoenicians were abruptly severed by the killing of Jezebel and her retainers and the suppression of Phoenician cults in Israel. The alliance with Judah could not survive the murder of King Ahaziah. The loss of these allies carried a heavy price. Israel was left militarily and politically isolated, and deprived of important revenues from trade. Moreover, the upheaval had disrupted normal internal administration. Whatever his merits as a soldier, Jehu did not have the capacity as a ruler to restore the cohesion and strength of the kingdom. It soon lay wide open to the growing power of Aram-Damascus (Syria), which had also had its coup, shortly before Jehu had come to power: the army officer Hazael had assassinated King Ben-hadad and seized the Damascus throne.

At first, however, it seemed as if both Jehu's Israel and Hazael's Syria would be crushed under the heel of Assyria. In 841 BC, the year after Jehu became king, a military expedition under the Assyrian emperor Shalmanezer III defeated Syria (though without taking Damascus), then turned westward through Israel as far as Mount Carmel, where tribute was accepted from Israel and Tyre. A black stone obelisk from Assyria depicts Jehu kneeling in homage before Shalmanezer. Laden with spoil the Assyrians returned to their country, and for the next thirty-five years were occupied with other parts of their empire.

Hazael of Aram-Damascus soon took advantage of this and renewed the war against isolated Israel, securing control of all Israelite territory east of the river Jordan and also much of Galilee. Towards the end of Jehu's reign the northern Hebrew kingdom had shrunk to little more than the hill-country of Ephraim round the capital, Samaria, and had become in effect an impotent vassal-state under Syrian domination. At one point Hazael's army came through Israel, reached as far as Gath in the coastal plain, and exacted tribute from Judah, whose king was Joash.

When Jehu died, after a reign of twenty-eight years, his son and successor, Jehoahaz (815–801), inherited a weak and truncated Israel, still subservient to Syria. Its armed forces had dwindled to 'fifty horsemen and ten chariots and ten thousand footmen'. (II Kings 13:7) But a decade later, in 806 BC, Assyria reappeared on the scene, now under King Adad-nariri III, whose army swept through northern Syria and mauled the Syrian forces. This time Damascus surrendered, and Syria had to accept vassal status, with heavy annual payment of tribute.

According to Assyrian instructions Israel (still called 'The House of Omri') also paid tribute, as did Edom and Philistia. In spite of that the Assyrian invasion was greeted with great relief in Samaria, since it put an end to the Syrian pressure: '. . . the Lord gave Israel a saviour, so that they escaped from the hand of the Syrians; and the people of Israel dwelt in their homes as formerly'. (II Kings 13:5) The Assyrians withdrew because of their growing power-struggle with a new challenger, the kingdom of Urartu (Ararat) in the mountainous region to their north. The Assyrian presence would not reassert itself in the area for the next half-century. It would then spell doom for the kingdom of Israel.

Jehoahaz was succeeded by his son Joash (or Jehoash) (801–786 BC). He was able to recover lost ground, taking advantage of the blow Syria had suffered from the Assyrians. Success was predicted for him by the aged and dying prophet Elisha. When the king went to visit him, Elisha made Joash shoot an arrow through a window facing to the east, saying that was a symbol of victory against Aram. However, when the king was asked to strike the ground with his remaining arrows and did so three times, Elisha saw in this a sign that he would win three battles, but would not altogether overcome the enemy, as would have happened had he struck the ground five or six times. In the resumed war against Ben-hadad II, the son and heir of Hazael, Joash recovered Israelite territory and towns that had been in Syrian occupation.

Joash was provoked by his contemporary, King Amaziah of Judah, into a rather pointless war between the two kingdoms. The forces of Israel defeated those of Judah in a battle at Beth-shemesh, after which Joash partly destroyed the northern wall of Jerusalem, took hostages and collected a payment of silver and gold. This episode confirms that at this time Israel had regained enough military strength to push back the Syrians and to dominate Judah. The recovery ushered in the long and fruitful reign of Joash's son and successor Jeroboam II (786–746 BC).

EVENTS IN JUDAH

When Ahaziah the young king of Judah had gone north to join his kinsman Jehoram of Israel in the earlier war against Aram-Damascus, the control of affairs in Jerusalem had been left in the hands of his mother Athaliah. A princess of the house of Omri, she was a strong-willed and ambitious woman, thirsting for the exercise of power. On hearing that Ahaziah had been killed in Jehu's uprising, Athaliah had the royal offspring in Judah put to death, and seized the throne for herself. The only one to escape was her grandson Jehoash (or Joash), the infant son of King Ahaziah. He was hidden in the Temple by his aunt, who was married to Jehoiada the high priest.

In the roster of Hebrew rulers Athaliah (842–837 BC) has two distinctions. She was the only woman to occupy the throne, and the only monarch in the kingdom of Judah who was not a descendant of David. The Bible maintains a disapproving silence about the events of her six-year reign, except for the damning fact that she had brought with her the Baal-cult fashionable in her native Samaria, and had built a temple for it in the grounds of the Jerusalem palace.

The boy Jehoash was secretly reared in the Temple. When he was seven years old, the high priest conspired with the officers of the palace guard to have him crowned. Under the protection of the guards coming off duty on the Sabbath, the ceremony was publicly performed in front of the Temple. Hearing the sound of trumpets and the shouts of acclamation, the queen ran through the gate from the palace to the

Temple enclosure. When she grasped what was happening, she shouted 'treason! treason', and turned to flee. The soldiers seized her, took her back to the palace and put her to death. The pagan temple and its effigies were destroyed by the crowd and the Baal-priest Mattan killed at his altar. The boy-king was ushered into the palace and seated on the throne. He reigned for thirty-eight years (837–800 BC). While the high priest Jehoiada was alive the king remained under his influence. Jehoash ordered extensive renovations to the Temple, which had fallen into disrepair. The work was financed through a fund-raising drive by the priests and Levites throughout the kingdom. The proceeds were deposited, together with individual donations, in a large chest at the entrance to the Temple, under the joint control of the king and the high priest. After the contractors were paid, the gold and silver left over were used to replace the Temple vessels that had been rendered impure through use in the worship of Baal.

With the death of the aged Jehoiada, the influence of the priesthood at the court waned, and more secular and cosmopolitan circles came to the fore. Jehoiada's son Zechariah, one of the leading priests, vehemently denounced the king for religious backsliding, and accused him of reviving pagan practices. The resentful king had him condemned and stoned to death as an agitator. The Bible rightly charges that this was an act of ingratitude to the late high priest, who had been the king's protector and mentor from his childhood.

The weakness of both Hebrew kingdoms at this time was underlined by the invading Syrian expedition led by Hazael which cut through the kingdom of Israel and reached the city of Gath. It was headed off from marching into Judah only by the payment of a crippling tribute. Jehoash almost emptied the royal treasury and that of the Temple in order to find the amounts of gold and silver that were demanded. This display of military impotence, together with the antagonism aroused by the killing of the priest Zechariah, provoked the assassination of Jehoash by two palace officials. He was succeeded by his son Amaziah (800–783 BC).

As soon as he was firmly established on the throne, the new ruler executed his father's assassins. The Bible stresses that he did not harm their offspring, in accordance with the law that 'the fathers shall not be put to death for the children, or the children be put to death for the fathers; but every man shall die for his own sin'. (II Chronicles 25:4) This principle set out in the Book of Deuteronomy (Deuteronomy 24:16) was characteristic of the progressive social legislation evolved by the

Hebrew spirit. It was meant to put an end to the family and community blood-feuds of an older tradition and to stress the responsibility of the individual for his actions.

Aram-Damascus was now in decline and Amaziah considered the time was propitious to reassert the sway of Judah over the southern desert kingdom of Edom. He marched his army south through Hebron and Arad, and delivered a blow to the Edomites in the 'valley of Salt', the desolate Aravah rift below the Dead Sea. He then 'took Sela by storm'. The Hebrew word *sela* means 'rock', and some scholars identify this place name with the inaccessible and extraordinary Edomite city cut out of the red sandstone cliffs some ninety kilometres south-east of the Dead Sea. It was later called Petra by the Greeks, and became the capital of the Nabateans, a remarkable and skilled people, who settled in the deserts of the Negev and southern Jordan.

Elated by this military success Amaziah rashly sought a quarrel with Israel, then ruled by Joash of the house of Jehu. The Book of Chronicles refers to a specific issue that provoked the dispute. For the Edomite campaign, Amaziah decided to augment his own force with mercenaries from Israel, and so hired some. His religious counsellors, however, warned the king that the Lord would view with disfavour the use of elements from the northern kingdom. He accordingly thought it prudent to dispense with their services – and forfeit the silver he had already paid them. On their way back to their homes in the hills of Ephraim, the disgruntled men did a fair amount of killing and looting on their own account. Amaziah flew into a rage when he returned from his battles in Edom and heard of the havoc they had wrought.

Whether Amaziah's judgement was impaired by over-confidence or anger, his challenge to his northern neighbour proved to be disastrous. He sent word to the king of Israel: 'Come, let us look one another in the face.' The reply was contemptuous. Quoting a parable about a thistle trying to measure up to a cedar of Lebanon, Joash said: 'You have indeed smitten Edom, and your heart has lifted you up. Be content with your glory, and stay at home; for why should you provoke trouble, so that you fall, you and Judah with you?' (II Kings 14:8–10) Since Amaziah would not climb down, Joash marched into Judah. In the battle at Beth-shemesh in the Judean foothills, Amaziah was roundly defeated and taken captive. Joash entered Jerusalem, smashed down part of its northern fortifications, took the treasures of the Temple and the palace as booty, and returned to Samaria with a group of hostages.

Amaziah paid the penalty for this humiliating experience: a revolt against him broke out in Jerusalem and he fled to the city of Lachish, where he was killed. His son Uzziah (also called Azariah) came to the throne as a youth of sixteen. Like his older contemporary, Jeroboam II of Israel, Uzziah was to enjoy a long and prosperous reign, lasting for over forty years (783–742 BC).

9

The Eighth-Century Resurgence

In the eighth century BC there was a marked upswing in the fortunes of the two Hebrew kingdoms, due to a combination of favourable circumstances. External pressures had been dramatically relaxed at the turn of the century. Israel's strongest and most aggressive neighbour, Syria, had been crippled by the invading Assyrian army of Adad-nariri III. Soon after the Assyrians had disappeared again from the vicinity, owing to distractions nearer home. To the south Egyptian might remained distant and dormant. In this power vacuum both Israelite kingdoms started to shake off their helplessness and go over to the offensive. Joash of Israel had been able to regain the territories lost to Syria, and Amaziah of Judah had started to reassert control over Edom.

This process of recovery surged forward during the parallel reigns of their respective sons, Jeroboam II of Israel and Uzziah of Judah – both of them among the ablest and most statesmanlike monarchs in Hebrew annals. By mid-century the divided nation enjoyed an internal stability, a material well-being, a territorial expansion and a regional importance that recalled the golden age of the monarchy under David and Solomon.

ISRAEL UNDER JEROBOAM II

Jeroboam II consolidated Israel's control of Trans-jordan down to the Dead Sea, and gained suzerainty over Aram-Damascus, so that the northern border extended to the kingdom of Hamath. Some of the lands liberated in Trans-jordan he divided among his friends and supporters. The group of feudal estate owners who evolved from these grants played an important part in later centuries.

Good relations were resumed between Jeroboam II and Uzziah of Judah after the disruption caused by the brief war between their fathers.

On the other hand the friendship and cooperation with the Phoenician cities of Tyre and Sidon, which had so roughly been broken by Jehu, were not restored in the reign of his descendant Jeroboam II, nor in fact during the rest of the history of the northern kingdom. Yet in spite of the loss of trade advantages that the Phoenician alliance had brought, living standards rose. The general level of prosperity was shown in the extent and the quality of the building projects carried out by Jeroboam II. He further developed the capital city of Samaria, and added to towns and fortifications elsewhere. The archaeological excavations at Hazor reveal that the buildings dating from the period of Jeroboam II were, to quote Professor Yadin, 'among the finest of the entire Israelite period'. Incidentally the dig also shows the destruction wrought by a great earthquake at that time (about 763 BC), vividly described by the contemporary prophet Amos:

> Shall not the land tremble on this account,
> and every one mourn who dwells in it,
> and all of it rise like the Nile,
> and be tossed about and sink again, like the Nile of Egypt?
> 'And on that day,' says the Lord God,
> 'I will make the sun go down at noon,
> and darken the earth in broad daylight. [Amos 8:8, 9]

Amos records that his ministry was carried out 'in the days of Uzziah' and 'of Jeroboam . . . two years before the earthquake'. His was the thankless task of preaching moral principle to a society enjoying the fruits of material prosperity under these two gifted royal statesmen.

Amos, a herdsman from the village of Tekoa, south of Bethlehem, was the first of the great classical or literary Hebrew prophets who appeared from the eighth to the sixth century BC. Like those who followed him, he was unimpressed by power and wealth and concerned only with moral and social values. Beneath the surface stability and affluence of Jeroboam's kingdom, Amos perceived the worm of decay, and was utterly fearless in his criticism. The poor, he complained, were oppressed, while the rich lived in luxury and corruption:

> You who afflict the righteous, who take a bribe,
> and turn aside the needy in the gate. [Amos 5:12]

Religious observance was a sham, based on formal ritual rather than on genuine devotion to God. He warned the privileged classes that they had built fine 'houses of hewn stone' – as the archaeologists found – but they would not dwell in them, and had planted vineyards but would not drink the wine.

With uncanny historical instinct he predicted that the sense of security in Israel was based on delusion, and that the State would be destroyed by its enemies.

> Woe to those who are at ease in Zion,
> and to those who feel secure on the mountain of Samaria. [Amos 6:1]

He promised, however, that the people would survive and rebuild its homeland.

It is little wonder that Amos' utterances did not endear him to the establishment. He seems to have based himself on Bethel, the main religious centre in the northern kingdom, where he had made his first prophetic appearance. The chief priest of the Bethel sanctuary, called Amaziah, sent a message to king Jeroboam accusing Amos of sedition. The prophet, he charged, preached that:

> Jeroboam shall die by the sword,
> and Israel must go into exile,
> away from his land. [Amos 7:11]

Apparently the authorities in Samaria were not much disturbed by the utterances of a troublesome preacher in Bethel, and failed to take action against him. The priest then addressed himself directly to Amos in the hope that he could be persuaded to leave: 'O seer, go, flee away to the land of Judah, and eat bread there, and prophesy there; but never again prophesy at Bethel, for it is the king's sanctuary, and it is a temple of the kingdom.' (Amos 7:12, 13) Amos retorted that he was not a professional prophet, as Amaziah's words implied; he was a man of the fields and pastures, but the Lord had called him away from his flocks of sheep to perform this mission. He repeated in even fiercer terms his prediction of the disaster to come.

Amos was closely followed by Hosea, who started to prophesy in the same vein towards the end of the reign of Jeroboam II and continued for some time thereafter. By then the prophetic warnings were no longer out of step with the times. Hosea's countrymen could not shrug it off when told that 'they sow the wind, and they shall reap the whirlwind'. (Hosea 8:7) After the death of Jeroboam II the kingdom of Israel disintegrated rapidly, and within a generation would come to a melancholy end.

JUDAH UNDER UZZIAH

The period covered by Uzziah, his son Jotham and his grandson Ahaz in Judah furnishes biblical scholars with a chronological headache. In the latter part of Uzziah's reign he contracted leprosy, which obliged him to withdraw from public life and live in quarantine in a 'separate house', probably outside the city walls. For the remainder of Uzziah's life his eldest son Jotham 'was over the household, governing the people of the land' – that is, he acted as regent, presumably in consultation with his father. It is difficult to know where the responsibility and the credit lay for what was done during this period of father-son rule. On Uzziah's death Jotham reigned in his own right – if indeed he outlived his father – and was succeeded by his son Ahaz. It is thus possible that Ahaz also acted for a while as regent. All dates for the overlapping reigns of these three kings are conjectural. The suggested dates are: Uzziah (783–742 BC); Jotham (as regent, 750–742; as king, 742–735); Ahaz (735–715).

The Book of Chronicles gives a theological reason for Uzziah's dread disease. According to this account the king entered the Temple with a censer in his hand in an attempt to burn incense on the small altar dedicated to this purpose. His way was barred by the high priest and a group of eighty stalwart priests. The high priest sternly demanded that the king withdraw at once, since incense burning was the exclusive prerogative of the Temple priesthood. Uzziah was furious at being balked. Suddenly the priests observed with horror that the signs of leprosy had appeared on the king's forehead, and he was hurried away at once. The moral seems to be that even a distinguished monarch was not immune from punishment for a sacrilegious deed.

Under Uzziah Judah extended its rule over adjacent areas to the south and west, as Israel under Jeroboam II did to the north and east. The whole of Edom was brought under subjection and the port of Ezion-geber reconstructed at the tip of the Negev. This brought Judah once more astride the trade routes from Arabia and the Red Sea area. Uzziah campaigned against the Philistines, dismantled the fortifications of Gath, Ashdod and Jabneh, and established new centres of Israelite settlement in the coastal plain. Judah was thus assured again of access to the Mediterranean. Raboth-ammon, the Ammonite capital in Transjordan, became a tribute-paying vassal. The marauding 'Arab' (nomad) tribes in the southern desert were subdued.

During the reigns of Jeroboam II and Uzziah the two kingdoms together held sway over an area roughly corresponding to that of David's empire.

In order to protect and control his expanded kingdom and the important caravan routes that went through it, Uzziah paid special attention to defence arrangements. The army was enlarged and reorganized under the direction of its commander, Hananiah, and re-equipped with shields, spears, helmets, coats of mail, bows and slings. These measures produced armed forces 'who could make war with mighty power, to help the king against the enemy'. (II Chronicles 26:13).

The fortifications of Jerusalem were strengthened and towers built 'at the Corner Gate and at the Valley Gate and at the Angle'. Special attention must have been given to the northern wall, where there were no natural defences corresponding to the steep ravines round the other three sides of the city. It was this northern wall that had been partly destroyed by Joash, king of Israel, in the reign of Uzziah's father Amaziah. Biblical scholars have been puzzled by the statement that 'In Jerusalem he made engines, invented by skilful men, to be on the towers and the corners, to shoot arrows and great stones.' (II Chronicles 26:15) At first glance this suggests that Uzziah's experts conceived the catapult and also designed a new type of bow. That is improbable, because they would certainly have been adopted by other armies of the period and evidence of them would have come to light in contemporary reliefs and inscriptions. The most feasible interpretation is that offered by Professor Yadin in his *The Art of Warfare in Biblical Lands*. According to him the reference is to special shielded platforms which Uzziah's engineers built on the tops of towers and city walls from which the defenders could fire their arrows and cast 'great stones' upon the heads of the assault troops below.

We are also told that Uzziah 'built towers in the wilderness'. (The biblical Hebrew verse recording this fact is the lyric of a popular song in modern Israel.) Archaeological remains have been found of the fortresses constructed in his time in the arid southern part of the country, no doubt to safeguard the trading routes, as well as the Israelite settlements that were fostered in the Negev. Among such strong-points are the fort at Ezion-geber, the one at Hurvat Uzza near Arad on the plateau overlooking the Dead Sea, and that at Kadesh-barnea, the oasis on the edge of the Sinai desert some ninety kilometres south of Gaza. These forts had casemate walls, not solid ones, indicating that their designers were less concerned about battering rams at these isolated spots than they would be in planning the defences of an important city.

The best preserved, and most interesting of Uzziah's desert citadels is the one at Kadesh-barnea, originally discovered in 1905. When the locality fell into Israel hands during the Sinai Campaign of 1956, the army was immediately followed by a team of archaeologists who examined all the sites in the area. They confirmed that this citadel belonged to the period of Uzziah, and not to that of the United Monarchy as had been thought at first. The rectangular building measures approximately forty-eight metres by thirty metres and has casemate walls with eight square towers, one at each corner and one in the middle of each side.

Uzziah had the rare distinction of being a Hebrew farmer-king, with a special interest in the development of agriculture in his realm. It is said that he 'hewed out many cisterns, for he had large herds, both in the Shephelah and in the plain, and he had farmers and vinedressers in the hills and in the fertile lands, for he loved the soil'. (II Chronicles 26:10)

While Uzziah's scriptural record was blemished by his intrusion into the Temple, Jotham, his son, was regarded as wholly meritorious. The kingdom continued to prosper under his guidance because 'he did what was right in the eyes of the Lord . . .' (II Chronicles 27:2) He is credited with defeating the Ammonites and exacting an annual tribute in silver, wheat and barley. He constructed the upper gate of the Temple, strengthened the city wall and added to the number of fortified towns outside Jerusalem. Since his reign partly merges with that of his father, it is difficult to tell whether these achievements are to be ascribed independently to him as king, or whether they refer to those already recorded in the account of the latter part of Uzziah's reign when Jotham was administering the kingdom as regent.

By contrast with Jotham, his son Ahaz is stamped as a bad king. He is denounced for indulging in pagan rites, and even accused of reviving the abominable practice of child-sacrifices, including that of his own son. To this religious relapse is attributed the decline that set in during his reign, and the series of reverses that left Judah a weak and shrunken vassal-state. The background was the reappearance in the area of Assyrian might. This time it had come to stay.

10

The Fall of Samaria

Assyria had emerged victorious from a long and confused struggle against rival powers. The dynamic Tiglath-pileser III (also called 'Pul' in the Bible) started a new dynasty in 745 BC and launched the greatest era of empire-building in Assyrian history. His armies marched westward to the Mediterranean coast, in the footsteps of Shalmanezer III a century earlier. But where his predecessors had plundered and returned, Tiglath-pileser conquered and colonized. The kingdoms battered into submission by his invincible war machine were annexed to the empire as provinces. Their ruling classes were deported, and peoples from other parts of the empire were brought in as settlers.

By 738 BC the Assyrian domain stretched from the river Tigris westward to Asia Minor and down as far as the Lebanese mountains. The kingdom of Hamath in northern Syria had been swallowed up, while tribute was exacted from Aram-Damascus, the kingdom of Israel, the Phoenician port cities and Arabia. According to Tiglath-pileser's inscriptions, in that same year he defeated a league of local kings headed by Azariah (i.e. Uzziah) of Judah, but surprisingly enough this event is not expressly mentioned in the Bible. The Assyrian menace may, however, explain the special effort made in Uzziah's reign to build up the army and defences of Judah.

The king of Israel mentioned in the Assyrian inscription as a vassal was Menahem (745–738 BC). After the death of Jeroboam II the stability established in his reign had again been gravely shaken, and the coup became the regular route to the throne of Israel. Jeroboam's son Zechariah (746–745 BC), the last of the Jehu dynasty, was assassinated six months after his accession by a certain Shallum, who seized power and 'reigned' for a month before being murdered in his turn by Menahem. The latter may have been the governor or commander in the old capital of Tirzah, from where he marched on Samaria to depose the usurper Shallum. To raise the thousand shekels of silver demanded as tribute by Tiglath-pileser, Menahem imposed a levy of fifty shekels on each of his more affluent subjects.

Menahem's son Pekahiah (738–737 BC) remained submissive to the Assyrian overlords. After two years he was slain and the throne seized by one of the army commanders, Pekah, son of Remaliah (737–732 BC). Pekah must have been serving in Trans-jordan at the time, as he carried out his coup with fifty troopers from Gilead.

It is known from Assyrian records that in 734 BC Tiglath-pileser pushed down the coastal plain through Phoenicia and Philistia as far as Gaza and the Egyptian border, where he left a garrison and turned back. This flanking movement must have frightened the local kings into organizing collective resistance. Pekah, King of Israel, formed an anti-Assyrian pact with Rezin, king of Aram-Damascus, and they received promises of support from the desert kingdoms of Ammon, Moab and Edom and the rulers of Gaza and Ashkelon in Philistia. King Ahaz of Judah refused to join the alliance. This meant that in a confrontation with Assyria, Israel and Aram-Damascus would be left exposed in the rear. Pekah and Rezin thereupon decided that Judah had to be brought into line, or at least neutralized. They invaded Judah with a combined force, inflicted a defeat on the army of Ahaz and besieged Jerusalem.

The vassals of Judah seized this opportune moment to break away. The Edomites regained territory in the Negev and captured part of Ezion-geber (Eilat). The Philistines too threw off the yoke of Judah, and pushed into the Judean foothills, taking Beth-shemesh and other border towns.

With his kingdom under attack from all sides, the desperate Ahaz sent messengers to Tiglath-pileser with a huge gift of gold and silver and said: 'I am your servant and your son. Come up, and rescue me from the hand of the king of Syria and from the hand of the king of Israel, who are attacking me.' (II Kings 16:7)

The Assyrian ruler promptly and effectively responded to the plea. He was being urged to do what he had probably planned to do anyway. In 733 BC his forces marched down from the north, broke through the fortified border of Israel at the northern end of the Jordan valley, and then fanned out, with units thrusting westwards through Galilee to the Mediterranean coast, south-westwards through Jezreel and southwards through Trans-jordan to the Dead Sea. Key fortified cities, like Hazor and Megiddo, were destroyed – the record is confirmed by the archaeological evidence. The extensive territory that was conquered was organized into three Assyrian provinces named Dor (the coastal district), Megiddo (Galilee) and Gilead (Trans-jordan). A number of the inhabitants were deported.

This reduced the kingdom of Israel to a small, truncated, vassal-state. Pekah did not survive the disaster. He was murdered by the son of Elah, Hoshea (732–724 BC), who was allowed to occupy the throne as an obedient Assyrian puppet.

The year after dismembering Israel, Tiglath-pileser rounded off his conquests in the region by occupying Damascus. Syria and the areas under its control were also incorporated into the empire as new Assyrian provinces. One of the wall reliefs in Tiglath-pileser's palace shows the inhabitants of the Syrian city of Ashtaroth, on the plateau of Bashan east of the Sea of Galilee, being hauled away into exile.

Having already placed itself under Assyrian protection, Judah remained intact for the time being. King Ahaz went to Damascus and paid homage to Tiglath-pileser. In order to raise tribute, he even dismantled some of the great bronze works in the courtyard of the Temple, such as the 'molten sea', and replaced the metal in part with stone. Yet during his visit to Damascus he was so taken with an altar he saw there that he had a scale model made of it and sent it to the high priest in Jerusalem with instructions to construct a replica and place it in front of the Temple.

THE END OF THE NORTHERN KINGDOM

In 727 BC Tiglath-pileser III died and was succeeded by his son Shalmanezer V. Encouraged by Egypt, Hoshea of Israel attempted a revolt against Assyrian control. His suicidal action lost him the throne and led to the crushing of what was left of his kingdom. Shalmanezer invaded Israel. Hoshea surrendered or was taken captive, and his fate is unknown. The Assyrians laid siege to Samaria. It held out for three years, then fell to Shalmanezer's successor, Sargon II. Sargon recorded that he rounded up 27,290 important inhabitants and transferred them to distant parts of his empire. According to the Bible the deportees were relocated in 'Halah, and on the Habor, the river of Gozan, and in the cities of the Medes'. (II Kings 17:6) (The 'cities of the Medes' refers to the province of Media, east of the Tigris river, which had only just been conquered by the Assyrians. Gozan and the Habor river lay to the west of the Tigris and of Nineveh.) The kingdom of Israel disappeared from the map, and was replaced by the new Assyrian province of Samaria, which included the coastal district of Dor. Implementing the imperial policy of population exchanges, Sargon brought in other settlers from Babylonia, and from Hamath in northern Syria. A few years later the population of Samaria was augmented by settlers from Arabia, who had also come under Assyrian domination. Out of this melting pot – the Israelites who had been allowed to remain, together with some of the indigenous Canaanite groups they had absorbed, and the large mixture of foreign deportee settlers – evolved the people who became known as the Samaritans.

11

The Age of Hezekiah

Hezekiah (715–687 BC) succeeded his father Ahaz when Judah was barely surviving on the fringe of the Assyrian empire. One of the most remarkable of the Hebrew kings, he set about creating the conditions for the continued existence, however precarious, of the remaining Hebrew state. Learning from the downfall of Israel, he kept a meek posture with the Assyrian authorities in the region, and gave them no reason to intervene in the internal affairs of the kingdom. The time he gained was put to good use.

Hezekiah's first concern was to restore the moral strength and religious conviction of his people. An end was put to the laxness and pagan ways tolerated in his father's reign. The Temple was repaired, cleansed and purified. The priests and Levites were reorganized, and their income assured from tithes. In Jerusalem, and throughout the kingdom, local pagan shrines were destroyed together with the images in them. Hezekiah then sent out messengers with a royal proclamation summoning the people to a great Passover festival in Jerusalem. He included in this invitation the towns and villages in the Assyrian province of Samaria that had been the northern kingdom of Israel. By this he hoped to heal the breach that had split the nation after Solomon's death and also to restore the Davidic dynasty, Jerusalem, and the Temple as the focus for the whole Hebrew nation. Hezekiah's attempt failed. Most of the Samaritan Israelites did not respond to his invitation, for two reasons: the age-old tribal jealousy; and Assyria's shrewd move in restoring and reorganizing the Bethel sanctuary.

The Book of Chronicles deals at length with Hezekiah's religious reforms, and commends him for doing 'what was good and right and faithful before the Lord his God'. (II Chronicles 31:20)

THE PROPHET ISAIAH

Hezekiah received powerful support from the greatest of the classical Hebrew prophets, Isaiah the son of Amoz. Isaiah believed passionately that only true faith in God and a return to the purity of the Mosaic creed could save what he called 'a sinful nation, a people laden with iniquity, offspring of evildoers'. (Isaiah 1:4) The Lord did not want sacrifices and empty rituals, he preached, but that each man should 'cease to do evil, learn to do good'. (Isaiah 1:16–17)

In the Book of his name Isaiah related that at the age of twenty-five he had a vision of God in the year that king Uzziah died. He heard the voice of the Lord saying, 'whom shall I send, and who will go for us?' Isaiah replied: 'Here am I, send me.' (Isaiah 6:8) For nearly half a century after that day Isaiah devoted himself in Jerusalem to his prophetic vocation, serving as a respected counsellor to three successive kings: Jotham, Ahaz and Hezekiah. The message he left behind forms the most sublime religious poetry in the whole of the Old Testament.

When Pekah of Israel and Rezin of Aram-Damascus invaded Judah in the reign of Ahaz, there was panic in Jerusalem, and the king sought Isaiah's counsel. The prophet reassured him: 'Take heed, be quiet, do not fear, and do not let your heart be faint because of these two smoldering stumps of firebrands . . .' (Isaiah 7:4) Against Isaiah's advice, however, Ahaz turned to the Assyrian ruler Tiglath-pileser III for help, bartering in exchange the independence of Judah. Thirty years later, Isaiah's opinion would similarly be disregarded by King Hezekiah. But much was to happen before then.

Hezekiah did not content himself with moral rearmament alone. He worked steadily to develop the efficiency of the kingdom and the strength of its defences, especially the capacity of Jerusalem to withstand a siege. The city ramparts were built up with towers and an outer wall. An abundance of weapons were provided for the army. Fighting commanders were appointed for the reserves. They were brought together and addressed by the king in front of the city gates: 'Be strong and of good courage, Do not be afraid or dismayed before the king of Assyria and all the horde that is with him; for there is one greater with us than with him.' (II Chronicles 32:7)

The most important step the king took in Jerusalem concerned its water supply in time of siege. Hezekiah 'made the pool and the conduit and brought the water into the city'. (II Kings 20:20) The spring of Gihon, the city's main water source, emerged from a cave outside the eastern wall. Hezekiah had a three-hundred-and-thirty-metre tunnel hewn underneath the wall to tap the water from the spring and discharge it into a reservoir inside the city called the Pool of Siloam (or Shiloah). The mouth of the cave was then sealed up to protect the source and deny the water to a besieging force. The tunnel remains intact to the present day. An accidental discovery in 1880 strikingly confirmed the biblical account of Hezekiah's engineering achievement. The lower part of an inscription was found on the rock wall of the tunnel. It was written in classical Hebrew of the period of Hezekiah, and it describes how two teams of miners worked from opposite ends and met in the middle. This 'Siloam inscription' now preserved in the Istanbul Museum, reads in English translation as follows:

. . . And this was the way in which it was cut through: while . . . [were] . . still axe[s], each man toward his fellow, and while there were still three cubits to be cut through [there was heard] the voice of a man calling to his fellow, for there was an overlap in the rock on the right [and on the left]. And when the tunnel was driven through, the quarrymen hewed [the rock], each man toward his fellow, axe against axe; and the water flowed from the spring toward the reservoir for 1,200 cubits, and the height of the rock above the head[s] of the quarrymen was 100 cubits.

In the latter part of Sargon's reign there had already been unrest among the subject people in the Assyrian empire, stimulated by two other powers – Babylonia and Egypt. In 712 BC, early in the reign of Hezekiah, Sargon crushed a revolt in the Philistine port city of Ashdod and annexed it. His inscriptions indicate that Judah, Edom and Moab were also implicated, but quickly submitted to him to save themselves. According to the Book of Isaiah the leaders of the revolt had relied on promises of support from Egypt, then ruled by the Pharaoh Shabaku, founder of the twenty-fifth (Ethiopian) dynasty. At the time the prophet Isaiah had appeared in public 'naked and barefoot', to dramatize his warning that Egypt would also submit to the might of Assyria, and desert the small nations that had relied on her. These nations would say: 'Behold, this is what has happened to those in whom we hoped and to whom we fled for help to be delivered from the king of Assyria! And we, how shall we escape?' (Isaiah 20:6)

The spirit of resistance sprang up again in the empire on the death of

Sargon in 705 BC and the accession of his son Sennacherib. It was probably in this atmosphere that Hezekiah concentrated on defence measures, including the fortifications and water supply for Jerusalem. Having decided that the time was ripe to throw off the Assyrian yoke, he worked to form a common front with mutinous Philistine cities and others. Ashkelon openly raised the banner of revolt. The people of Ekron joined, after deposing their king, Padi (who wished to remain a loyal vassal), and sending him in chains to Hezekiah in Jerusalem. A delegation from the king of Babylon arrived in Jerusalem carrying letters and presents. Hezekiah gave them a warm welcome and personally showed them round the palace and the treasure houses. Isaiah warned his royal master that the association with the Babylonians would bring calamity in the future. Hezekiah shrugged his shoulders and said to himself, 'Why not, if there will be peace and security in my day?' (II Kings 20:19) Above all, Isaiah once more protested against the misplaced confidence in Egyptian support. The involvement in the power-politics of the region was for him a perilous substitute for reliance on God:

> 'Woe to the rebellious children,' says the Lord
>   'who carry out a plan, but not mine;
> and who make a league but not of my spirit . . .
>   Woe to those who go down to Egypt for help
> and rely on horses,
>   who trust in chariots because they are many
> and in horsemen because they are very strong,
>   but do not look to the Holy One of Israel
> or consult the Lord! . . .
>   The Egyptians are men, and not God;
> and their horses are flesh, and not spirit.' [Isaiah 30:1; 31:1, 3]

For the first three years of his reign Sennacherib was fully occupied in restoring Assyrian domination in Mesopotamia. In 701 BC he was free to reassert Assyrian power along the Mediterranean littoral. His cohorts swept through northern Syria and down along the Phoenician coast. An Egyptian army marched up through Philistia to meet them and was routed on the Sorek river (near the present Rishon le-Zion). The two Philistine cities of Ekron and Ashkelon surrendered, and the Assyrian force turned inland to ravage the towns of the Shephelah, the foothills area of Judah. Sennacherib's inscriptions claim that forty-six towns in Judah fell to him, with many captives and a great deal of booty.

The main battle took place at the strongly fortified city of Lachish, about half-way between Hebron in the hills and Ashkelon on the coast. Among the stone wall-reliefs discovered in 1849 in Sennacherib's palace at Nineveh, one series (now in the British Museum) is devoted to detailed scenes from the siege and capture of Lachish – one of the most important and instructive war documentaries to have survived from ancient times. The excavations carried out at the site of Lachish up to 1938 confirm the strength of the defences that were overcome by assault after a bitter struggle.

As for Hezekiah, Sennacherib records: 'I imprisoned [him] in Jerusalem, his residence, like a bird in a cage.' Hezekiah was indeed in a hopeless position, and sent a humble message to the Assyrian monarch at Lachish, seeking surrender terms: 'I have done wrong . . . whatever you impose on me I will bear.' (II Kings 18:14) To meet the tribute exacted from him, Hezekiah had to drain the official treasury and that in the Temple of all their gold and silver, and even to strip the Temple doors of their gold covering.

Sennacherib was not satisfied. He despatched three top aides to Jerusalem with a large force, to demand the complete surrender of the city. The appointments held by the three officials are given in the Bible as the *Tartan* (commander-in-chief), the *Rabsaris* (master of the eunuchs) and the *Rabshakeh* (probably chief of the royal staff). The spokesman was the Rabshakeh, clearly a clever and articulate man who had a command of languages, including Hebrew.

The Assyrian officials took up their position below the eastern wall near the Gihon spring, and demanded to see the king. Three of Hezekiah's officials came out to parley with them: Eliakim the head of the royal household; Shebnah the palace secretary; and Joah the recorder. They had to listen to some tough talk – in Hebrew – from the Rabshakeh in the name of his imperial master. King Hezekiah should not delude himself that the city would be able to withstand an Assyrian attack. What ground was there for such a hope? 'Do you think that mere words are strategy and power for war? On who do you now rely, that you have rebelled against me? Behold, you are relying now on Egypt, that broken reed of a staff, which will pierce the hand of any man who leans on it.' (II Kings 18:20, 21)

At this point the Israelite deputation requested that the Rabshakeh speak to them in Aramaic, the diplomatic and commercial language of the region, rather than in Hebrew, the spoken tongue of the soldiers manning the wall above them who were avidly following the exchange. The Rabshakeh grasped the point, and promptly exploited it by continuing with a demagogic appeal addressed directly to the onlookers. The message from his master, he said, was "Do not let Hezekiah deceive you, for he will not be able to deliver you out of my hand." (II Kings 18:29) As for divine protection, all the other countries conquered by Assyria, including Samaria, had not been saved by their gods – why should Jerusalem be any different? If they submitted and made their peace with the king of Assyria, they would have no cause for concern; they would not be killed, but would be taken away to a 'land like your own land, a land of grain and wine, a land of bread and vineyards, a land of olive trees and honey . . .' (II Kings 18:32)

The men on the wall kept silent, as they had been instructed to do. Hezekiah's agitated officials then returned to report to the king. In great dismay Hezekiah sent them to consult Isaiah, saying: 'This day is a day of distress, of rebuke, and of disgrace . . .' (II Kings 19:3) The prophet sent back a staunch message. The king should stand firm, and the Lord would cause the Assyrians to withdraw to their own country, where their ruler would fall by the sword.

Having failed to obtain the surrender of Jerusalem by bluster, the Rabshakeh went back to report to Sennacherib and seek fresh instructions. He found that after the fall of Lachish, the Assyrian king was busy attacking the city of Libnah in the foothills a few kilometres to the north. Sennacherib sent back messengers with a threatening letter to Hezekiah. Once again it was Isaiah who counselled faith and defiance. 'Therefore, thus says the Lord concerning the king of Assyria, He shall not come into this city or shoot an arrow there, or come before it with a shield or cast up a siege mound against it. By the way that he came, by the same he shall return, and he shall not come into this city, says the Lord.' (II Kings 19:32, 33)

That night, according to the biblical account, the angel of the Lord went forth and killed a great number of Assyrian soldiers. A more mundane explanation may have been the outbreak of an epidemic in the Assyrian camp. Sennacherib may also have received news of trouble at home. Isaiah's words imply as much: 'he shall hear a rumour and return to his own land'. Whatever the reasons, Sennacherib broke off the campaign in Judah and returned to Nineveh. It may well be that the threats conveyed through the Rabshakeh and in his own letter to Hezekiah were bluff, and that he did not really intend to commit his forces to a long and costly siege if Hezekiah did not hand over Jerusalem. However, as far as Hebrew tradition is concerned, the city was saved by a divine miracle. Isaiah's role in this deliverance marks his last appearance in the biblical narrative. He must have died some time in the later years of Hezekiah's reign.

Jerusalem had been spared, but other cities in the kingdom had not, and so Sennacherib's expedition had served its main purpose. The bid for independence by Judah and certain other small states in the area had been crushed, and they reverted to the role of docile vassals. Nothing more is recorded about the rest of Hezekiah's reign, though shortly before the mention of his death, there is a flashback, with a human touch, to an episode in an earlier year when Hezekiah was near death. He fell critically ill from infected sores or boils – and was cured by a fig poultice prescribed by Isaiah!

THE REIGN OF MANASSEH

The next king of Judah, Hezekiah's son Manasseh (687–642 BC), succeeded to the throne at the age of twelve. By accepting Assyrian domination without demur, he provided Judah with nearly half a century of uneventful existence, and of steady recovery from the havoc of Sennacherib's campaign. In fact Manasseh had little option. In the first half of the seventh century BC, the Assyrian empire reached its zenith, and resistance to it would have been suicidal.

Sennacherib was assassinated by two of his sons while at prayer in his temple at Nineveh, and was succeeded by a younger son, the dynamic Esarhaddon (680–669 BC). In 671 Esarhaddon invaded Upper Egypt, captured Memphis, the ancient capital, seized the royal family and installed Assyrian district governors. His son and successor, Asshurbanipal (668–627 BC), suppressed an Egyptian rebellion and consolidated Assyrian control. An uprising in Babylonia in 652 BC was quelled after several years of struggle. Though surrounded by enemies and hated by its subject peoples, Assyria was now the undisputed master of the Near East. Manasseh appears in an Assyrian list of twenty-two kings who supplied Esarhaddon with building materials, and he is again named, by Asshurbanipal, as one of the vassals who assisted in the Egyptian campaign.

Within the kingdom Manasseh abandoned his father Hezekiah's policy of religious reform, and relapsed into the lax and permissive attitudes of his grandfather Ahaz. The local 'high places' Hezekiah had banned sprang into use again. The practices of pagan cults revived. It was said that the rite of child-sacrifice reappeared in the Hinnom valley, just outside the city walls of Jerusalem. Even the Temple precincts were not immune from profane altars and images.

To some extent the relapse was due to Assyrian influence. Conquered peoples tend to copy the ways of their conquerors. In this case deference was shown to the deities of the overlord, and there was an intrusion of the astrology and magic prevalent in Assyrian cults. Manasseh 'practised soothsaying and augury and sorcery, and dealt with mediums and with wizards'. (II Chronicles 33:6) Prophetic voices were raised in warning. The Lord, they cried, 'will wipe Jerusalem as one wipes a dish, wiping it and turning it upside down'. (II Kings 21:13)

According to the Book of Chronicles, Manasseh was carried off to Nineveh in chains, but repented and was restored to his throne by the Lord and promptly abolished the religious abuses. The Book of Kings makes no mention of such a change of heart; it indicates that the reform movement did not start until the reign of Josiah. Manasseh's son Amon (642–640 BC) is also charged with irreligious practices, for which he was murdered by anonymous palace officials. They in turn were condemned to death, and Amon's son Josiah (640–609 BC), while still a boy, was installed on the throne.

12

Judah: The Last Phase

osiah is regarded as one of the outstanding kings of Judah, and his
reign as the last interlude of greatness before the end of the kingdom.
At the age of eighteen, he started a religious reform programme. The
first step was to clean out and repair the Temple. He instructed
Hilkiah the high priest that the money collected from the public by the
gatekeepers should be handed to the builders, carpenters and masons:
'But no accounting shall be asked from them . . . for they deal honestly.'
(II Kings 22:7) Hilkiah said to Shaphan, the palace secretary who had
brought the king's message, that in the course of the work, 'the book
of the law' had been found in the Temple. (This was probably a scroll
containing an early version of the Book of Deuteronomy.) Shaphan
brought the book to the king and read it out to him. Josiah was overcome with emotion, and deeply disturbed to find how far religious life in
the kingdom had strayed from the precepts in the sacred work. The high
priest, the secretary and others were sent to consult the esteemed
prophetess Huldah, wife of the keeper of the royal wardrobe. She
predicted that the wrath of the Lord would be vented against the city
and its inhabitants for their evil deeds. Josiah thereupon called a great
assembly in the Temple including 'the priests and the prophets, all the
people, both small and great', and solemnly read the whole book aloud
to them. The assembly then joined him in a covenant with the Lord to
observe all that was written in the work.

This discovery gave impetus to a purge of pagan practices and objects
more sweeping even than that of the young king's great-grandfather,
Hezekiah. The altars, the vessels and the images in the Temple dedicated 'for Baal, for Asherah and for all the host of heaven' were burnt in
the Kidron valley. Idolatrous priests at local shrines in the country were
deposed. The building in the Temple compound used by male cult prostitutes was destroyed. 'High places' were defiled by scattering human

bones on them. The spot called Topheth in the valley of Hinnom was also defiled, 'that no one might burn his son or his daughter as an offering to Molech'. (II Kings 23:10)

These measures had political overtones. They showed that Judah had substantially recovered its independence, and that the king was not afraid to antagonize the crumbling Assyrian colossus. Josiah eliminated from the Temple every evidence of Assyrian worship of the celestial bodies, 'the sun, and the moon, and the constellations'. (II Kings 23:5) This included burning the figures of horses and chariots that had been erected in previous reigns at the entrance to the Temple in honour of the Assyrian sun-god. What was even more significant, Josiah extended his reforms to the former northern kingdom of Israel, now the Assyrian province of Samaria, indicating that Judah virtually controlled that territory.

The climax of the religious revival was a great Passover feast in Jerusalem, to which the whole country was invited, as well as the Israelite population left in Samaria. The ceremonies were carried out strictly according to 'the book of the covenant' found in the Temple. Thousands of animals were offered as sacrifices. 'For no such passover had been kept since the days of the Judges . . .' (II Kings 23:22)

THE FALL OF NINEVEH

Judah's regained freedom was a by-product of the fresh struggle taking place between the great powers of the Near East. Egypt had freed itself from Assyria in the last years of the reign of Asshurbanipal. After his death in 627 BC, the vast and over-extended empire started to disintegrate, and within the astonishing span of two decades it collapsed and disappeared, never to arise again. The joint agents of its downfall were two neighbouring kingdoms that had been held in subjection: Babylonia, down-river to the south, and Media to the east. In 626 BC Babylonia revolted, defeated an Assyrian army and resumed its independence. After twelve more years of erosion in Assyria, the Medes took by storm the original Assyrian capital city of Asshur on the Tigris river, south of the new capital, Nineveh. Two years later, in 612 BC, Nineveh itself fell in a combined onslaught by the Babylonians and Medes, and was sacked. With the capture of Haran in northern Syria, in 610 BC, the last Assyrian bastion was wiped out, and the mighty empire that had dominated and terrorized the Near East came to an abrupt end. The general exultation in the region is expressed by Nahum, the contemporary Hebrew prophet in 'An Oracle concerning Nineveh':

> Woe to the bloody city,
> all full of lies and booty –
> no end to the plunder!
> The crack of whip, and rumble of wheel,
> galloping horse and bounding chariot!
> Horsemen charging,
> flashing sword and glittering spear,
> hosts of slain,
> heaps of corpses,
> dead bodies without end . . .
> All who hear the news of you
> clap their hands over you
> For upon who has not come
> your unceasing evil?
>
> [Nahum 3:1–3, 19]

In the Mesopotamian death-struggle Egypt played a curious game – by joining forces with Assyria against its challengers from about 616 BC onwards. There was a balance-of power logic to this unexpected axis. Egypt had no more to fear from Assyria; on the contrary it saw a chance to regain its sway over Palestine and Syria. This design could be thwarted by the resurgent power of Babylonia. In 609 BC when the Assyrians were making a last-ditch stand in northern Syria, an Egyptian army under Pharaoh Neco marched up from the south to assist them.

King Josaiah mustered his forces to intercept the Egyptian troops at Megiddo. In the hope of avoiding a fight, the Pharaoh sent a message to Josiah, saying: 'What have we to do with each other, king of Judah? I I am not coming against you this day, but against the house with which I am at war.' (II Chronicles 35:21) Josiah would not be deterred. Presumably he feared that Assyrian rule would still be salvaged or that it might be replaced by Egyptian rule. In the ensuing battle his army was defeated and the king himself fatally wounded by an arrow. He was taken in his chariot to Jerusalem where he died. The Bible extols him as the most righteous of all the Hebrew kings, 'who turned to the Lord with all his heart and all his soul and with all his might, according to all the law of Moses'. (II Kings 23:25)

With Josiah's defeat and death Judah's independence was ended. For the remaining twenty-two years of its existence, the kingdom was helplessly caught between the contending ambitions of Egypt and Babylonia. After the battle of Megiddo Judah was for a while within the Egyptian orbit. Josiah was succeeded at first by his son Jehoahaz (609 BC), but three months later he was deposed and carried off by the Egyptians, who replaced him with his more cooperative brother Jehoiakim (609–598 BC). A heavy tribute of gold and silver was exacted, and the new king raised it by a tax on his subjects.

In 605 BC, when Judah had been an Egyptian vassal state for over three years, the army of Neco was decisively defeated by the new Babylonian ruler Nebuchadnezzar II at the battle of Carchemish, on the upper Euphrates river. In the following year Nebuchadnezzar marched southward into Philistia, smashed resistance from the city of Ashkelon, and reached the 'Brook of Egypt' (El-Arish). Within a few years Judah had shifted from the Assyrians through the Egyptians to the Babylonian orbit.

'Mesopotamia' is a Greek name meaning 'the land between the rivers' – that is, the Tigris and the Euphrates. Assyria occupied the upper and more mountainous part of this region. Its lower part, an immensely fertile irrigated plain, was Babylonia. The Neo-Babylonian empire that emerged from the collapse of the Assyrian empire quickly reached its highest level under Nebuchadnezzar II (606–562 BC). Its capital city, Babylon, stretched a long way by the east bank of the Euphrates, and its palaces, temples and city walls rivalled those of Nineveh in size and splendour. The 'hanging gardens' that spread across the rooftops of the vast royal palace were included by the Greeks among the seven wonders of the world. In affluence, in art and architecture, in the science of astronomy, in military skills, the Babylonians were unexcelled during their brief golden age.

Towards the end of the seventh century BC a Semitic people, the Chaldeans, became the dominant group in Babylonia, and Nebuchadnezzar belonged to a new Chaldean dynasty. In the Bible 'Chaldean' and 'Babylonia' are used as interchangeable names.

For the small Hebrew nation, clinging to the remnant of its statehood in Judah, the Babylonians went through rapid changes of aspect. Within a quarter of a century they appeared at first as liberators from Assyrian tyranny; then as conquerors and destroyers; and finally as the setting for exile. Judah might have survived longer under another king like Manasseh, meekly accepting subjection as a fact of life and making the best of it. But national pride and the spirit of freedom had been revived in Josiah's reign, and the thirst for independence eventually impelled his son Jehoiakim to disastrous policies. As before, ideas of revolt were encouraged by Egypt. Opinion within the kingdom was sharply divided between hawks and doves, between the faction headed by the king and his circle, who dreamt of defying Babylon, and those who thought such a course reckless. Jeremiah was the most vocal exponent of submission to Babylon.

THE PROPHET JEREMIAH

Jeremiah and Isaiah were the two giants among the classical Hebrew prophets. They lived in Jerusalem a century apart, and each was directly drawn into the fateful political events of his time. Jeremiah was born in the village of Anathoth five kilometres north-east of Jerusalem, the son of a local priest. About 627 BC, when King Josiah was on the throne, Jeremiah felt the call from the Lord to follow the vocation of a prophet. He was then about eighteen years of age.

He no doubt approved of Josiah's religious reformation, but became such a bitter and outspoken critic of Josiah's son Jehoiakim that he was in constant trouble with the authorities. The prophet's main target was the religious and moral corruption that had crept in again after Josiah's death. Soon after Johoiakim had been put on the throne by the Egyptians, Jeremiah addressed a crowd of worshippers in the Temple courtyard and swore that God would destroy the sanctuary itself if they did not mend their ways. He was seized by some of the priests and worshippers, and might have been killed if he had not been rescued and befriended by an important court official, Ahikam, whose father had been the royal scribe to Josiah.

Unrepentant, Jeremiah continued to denounce the whole establishment from the king downwards, and to predict destruction by Babylon. Dramatically smashing an earthenware jar, he shouted out to his audience: 'Thus says the Lord of hosts: So will I break this people and this city, as one breaks a potter's vessel, so that it can never be mended.' (Jeremiah 19:11)

Jeremiah's sermons and oracles were compiled into a book by his faithful disciple and scribe, Baruch. It came into the hands of the palace officials, who brought it to the king. He ordered the scroll to be read to him, and while that was being done, he hacked off the pieces in a rage and threw them on to the brazier in his chamber until the whole work was burned. He then ordered Jeremiah and Baruch to be arrested, but they had hidden themselves. Jeremiah promptly dictated the scroll over again to Baruch.

The prophet could not forgive the king for building himself a handsome new palace at a time of political crisis and economic hardship. The offence was compounded by the use of forced labour:

'Woe to him who builds his house by unrighteousness,
    and his upper rooms by injustice;
who makes his neighbour serve him for nothing,
    and does not give him his wages. . . .
Do you think you are a king
    because you compete in cedar?' [Jeremiah 22:13, 15]

Jeremiah gives details of the building. The remains of a palace matching his description and dating back to the period of Jehoiakim have been excavated at Ramat Rahel on the southern edge of Jerusalem. Its walls were made of fine ashlar blocks, and richly decorated capitals were lying in the ruins. One of the finds was a potsherd painted with a figure of a seated king. Some scholars believe it may well be a portrait of Jehoiakim.

For three years Jehoiakim kept a submissive posture towards the Babylonian authorities, while discreetly holding on to the Egyptian connection, and with his mind on rebellion at a suitable time. The moment seemed to have arrived in 601 BC, when Nebuchadnezzar advanced on Egypt, fought an inconclusive battle near its frontier, and withdrew again to Babylon. This was seen in the area as evidence that the Babylonian army was not invincible, and could be checked by Egyptian strength. Jeremiah warned against reliance on the Egyptians, as Isaiah had done in the days of Ahaz and Hezekiah:

'You shall be put to shame by Egypt
    as you were put to shame by Assyria.
From it too you will come away
    with your hands upon your head,
for the Lord has rejected those in whom you trust,
    and you will not prosper by them.' [Jeremiah 2:36, 37]

The king dismissed such counsels as defeatist. Spurred on by his militant advisers he 'turned and rebelled' against Nebuchadnezzar. For more than two years the Babylonian ruler took no direct action, being fully occupied elsewhere. In the meantime Judah was kept on the defensive by guerrilla raids from the territories of neighbours subject to

Babylon – Syria, Moab and Ammon – together with Babylonian garrison troops in the area.

If Jehoiakim concluded that nothing more serious would happen, he underrated the mighty adversary he had defied. In December 598 BC a Babylonian punitive expedition marched south to deal with the trouble in Judah. In the same month Jehoiakim died, or possibly was assassinated. His eighteen-year-old son Jehoiachin succeeded to the throne and was left to face the storm. The support expected from Egypt did not materialize – 'And the king of Egypt did not come again out of his land.' (II Kings 24:7) Within three months Jerusalem surrendered and the futile bid for freedom was over.

The young king gave himself up to Nebuchadnezzar, who carried him off to Babylon as a captive together with 'his mother, and his servants, and his princes, and his palace officials . . . and all the mighty men of valour, ten thousand captives, and all the craftsmen and the smiths; none remained, except the poorest people of the land'. (II Kings 24:12, 14) The palace and the Temple were stripped and their treasures taken as booty. Jehoiachin's uncle, Zedekiah, another of Josiah's sons, was installed as a puppet ruler (597–587 BC). A Babylonian inscription of the time states tersely that Nebuchadnezzar 'captured the city and took the king prisoner. A king of his own choice was set up in his midst'.

Zedekiah's status was anomalous, since his exiled nephew continued to be regarded both in Babylon and in Judah as the legitimate king. It is told in the Books of Kings and repeated in the Book of Jeremiah that thirty-seven years after Jehoiachin had been taken captive, he was shown special favour by a new ruler in Babylon, who 'graciously freed Jehoiachin king of Judah from prison; and he spoke kindly to him, and gave him a seat above the seats of the kings who were with him in Babylon. So Jehoiachin put off his prison garments'. (II Kings 25: 27–9) He was also given a regular maintenance grant. The records found in the basement of Nebuchadnezzar's palace mention that the 'king of Judah', his five sons and a list of other Judahites were among the captives issued with rations from the royal stores.

For a number of years Zedekiah unwillingly remained in the role of a vassal ruling over a shrunken Judah, with its economy crippled and vital elements of its population removed. In spite of the tragic national experience that had brought him to the throne, he clung to the hope of liberation. This longing was fanned by a revolt that flared up in Babylon in 594 BC, involving part of the army. It was suppressed by Nebuchad-nezzar, but unrest persisted in the Babylonian empire. Excited expecta-tions must have been aroused among the Jewish exiles; there is a suggestion in the Book of Jeremiah that two prophets were executed by the Babylonian authorities, who no doubt regarded their utterances as sedition. Jeremiah was indignant with prophets in Jerusalem who predicted that within two years Jehoiachin and the other exiles would return in triumph.

In this atmosphere Zedekiah started to conspire with other small vassal-states in the area. Envoys from the kings of Edom, Moab, Ammon, Tyre and Sidon came to Jerusalem for consultations. They were encouraged by a new pharaoh who had succeeded in Egypt.

Jeremiah campaigned with all his force against this dangerous trend, and denounced the courtiers and religious leaders who were inciting it. Given to making dramatic points with tangible symbols, he walked about Jerusalem with a yoke on his neck. The message was clear: accept Babylonian rule with resignation. In another striking Jeremiah meta-phor, a basket of good figs denoted the exiles whom God would preserve and bring back in his own time, while a basket of rotting fruit stood for the impatient king and his courtiers whom God would discard.

Jeremiah's preaching may have helped to restrain official policy. The proposed rebellion was quietly shelved, and Zedekiah thought it prudent to dispatch a delegation to Babylon with a message reaffirming his loyalty. Two of the members of the mission were known to Jeremiah, and with them he sent a letter to the community of exiles. It urged them to give up illusions about a quick return and to settle down with patience. What the Lord required of them, he wrote, was to 'build houses and live in them; plant gardens and eat of their produce. Take wives and have sons and daughters . . . multiply there, and do not decrease. But seek the welfare of the city where I have sent you into exile, and pray to the Lord on its behalf, for in its welfare you will find your welfare.' (Jeremiah 29: 6–7) This advice could hardly have been well received. One of the priests with the exiles wrote an angry protest to the high priest in Jerusalem, demanding that Jeremiah be punished.

Five years later, in 589 BC, the war party at the court prevailed and Zedekiah went into open revolt. Among the small states in the area,

Judah was joined only by Tyre and probably by Ammon. From Egypt the Pharaoh Hophra pledged himself to send troops in support.

The Babylonian response was swift and ruthless. Nebuchadnezzar's strategy was to wipe out the other fortified cities of Judah (some of which had been only partially but not completely destroyed in Nebuchadnezzar's previous invasion ten years earlier), leaving Jerusalem to the last. The assault on the capital would commence when it was isolated, cut off from potential Egyptian help. The other towns were captured and sacked one after another. The last to fall were Lachish and Azekah. Archaeological excavations at Beth-shemesh, Lachish, Beth-zur, Debir, Arad and En-gedi reveal evidence of the Babylonian destruction.

A unique find at Lachish, in a chamber adjacent to the city gate, was twenty-one ostraca (inscribed pottery fragments) dating from the time of King Zedekiah, shortly before the fall of the town. The writing, in black ink, is in early classical Hebrew script. Eighteen of them are letters from an army officer named Hoshaiah, commanding a nearby outpost, to his superior, Yaosh, commander of Lachish and the surrounding district. Hoshaiah had evidently read reports from high quarters in Jerusalem that had been transmitted through him. He expresses his unhappiness at the pessimistic tone of these despatches: 'And behold the words of the princes are not good, but to weaken our hands and to slacken the hands of the men who are informed about them . . . truly since your servant read the letters there has been no peace for your servant . . .'

One of the ostraca ends: 'We are watching for the fire signals of Lachish, according to all the signs my lord gave, because we do not see Azekah.' This may indicate that Azekah, a few kilometres north-east of Lachish, had already fallen to the Babylonian troops. When Lachish too was taken Nebuchadnezzar closed in on Jerusalem. The fate of Hoshaiah and Yaosh is not known; they may have been killed or captured in the general débacle.

After a short while the siege of Jerusalem was suddenly lifted and the Babylonian troops withdrew. Apparently they were diverted to meet a belated Egyptian relief force coming up from the south. One of the Lachish letters hints that Zedekiah's army commander may have paid an urgent visit to Egypt to hasten its intervention. There was a wave of joy in Jerusalem at the reprieve, with only Jeremiah stubbornly continuing to predict doom. The king must have felt some doubts about this turn of events, because he secretly sent for Jeremiah to hear his opinion. The prophet flatly told him that the Babylonians would be back. He was right; the Egyptian force was repulsed, and the siege resumed.

THE FALL OF JERUSALEM

Jerusalem heroically held out for at least another year (according to some scholars, two years). The end probably came in July 587 BC, when the food supplies were exhausted and the city was in the grip of famine. The Babylonian siege engines breached the wall and the attacking troops poured in. Under cover of darkness the king and some of his men escaped through the eastern gateway, and fled towards the Jordan river, perhaps hoping to find asylum in Trans-jordan. He was pursued, captured near Jericho and brought to the Babylonian regional head-quarters at Riblah in central Syria. Nebuchadnezzar treated him without pity. His sons were killed before his eyes; he was then blinded and taken in chains to Babylon, where he died.

A month later, Nebuzaradan, the commander of the Babylonian royal guard, arrived in Jerusalem with orders to destroy the city. Everything of value was pillaged, including the great bronze works in the Temple courtyard, which were hacked to pieces for the easier trans-port of the metal to Babylon. The Temple, the palace and the rest of the city were then put to the torch. The defence walls were smashed. The inhabitants were rounded up. The leading officials, priests and citizens were taken to Riblah, and there executed. A number of the rest (832, according to Jeremiah) were deported to Babylon.

The kingdom of Judah had come to a bloody end. Jewish statehood would not arise again until the Hasmonean period more than four centuries later.

With its capital and fortified towns wrecked, its economic life at a standstill, its leaders killed or exiled, Judah was annexed and turned into a minor province of the Babylonian empire. A certain Gedaliah, who had been one of Zedekiah's senior officials, was appointed as the local governor. He set himself up at Mizpah to the north of Jerusalem, where he was joined by remnants of the armed forces that had been scat-tered in the countryside. Gedaliah gathered and cared for destitute war refugees, tried to restore some measure of administration, and made a public appeal for restraint and obedience: 'Do not be afraid because of

Chaldean officials; dwell in the land, and serve the king of Babylon, and it shall be well with you.' (II Kings 25:24) He urged the peasant farmers who had been allowed to remain on the land as 'vinedressers and ploughmen' to go on cultivating their fields and to harvest the wine, fruit and oil.

Nebuchadnezzar may have received reports of Jeremiah's pacifist views and his tireless crusade against resistance. He gave orders that the holy man should be spared and treated well. Jeremiah was discovered among a group of shackled captives waiting at Ramah to be deported. The commander of the troops released him, provided him with food and gave him the choice of going voluntarily to Babylon or remaining in Judah. The prophet elected to join Gedaliah, whose father Ahikam had earlier protected him when he was in danger because of his provocative preaching.

A short while later Gedaliah was assassinated, together with his immediate entourage, by a group of hotheads led by a kinsman of the royal family, who regarded the governor as a collaborator. The assassins then fled from Mizpah, taking a number of hostages with them. Soldiers loyal to Gedaliah pursued them and managed to free the hostages, but the leader of the murder gang escaped. The loyalists returned not to Mizpah but to Geruth Chimham near Bethlehem, determined to secure asylum in Egypt for fear of punitive Babylonian action in Judah for the murder of Gedaliah, the Babylon-appointed governor. Babylonian reprisals were indeed swift and tough, and there was a further deportation from Judah. But the loyalist group had in the meantime fled to Egypt, much against the urgent advice of Jeremiah, who still ranted against the Egyptians – and they even took him with them, convinced no doubt that it was for his own safety. And it was presumably in Egypt that Jeremiah died some years later. There is a story that in Egypt the prophet berated an assembly of exiles for worshipping alien gods, and was told with some bitterness that their own God had not saved their homeland.

The feeling that God had turned against his chosen people found poignant expression in the Book of Lamentations (traditionally, though dubiously, attributed to Jeremiah):

> The Lord has become like an enemy,
>   he has destroyed Israel . . .
> the Lord has brought to an end in Zion
>   appointed feast and sabbath,

> and in his fierce indignation has spurned
>   king and priest.
> The Lord has scorned his altar,
>   disowned his sanctuary. [Lamentations 2:5–7]

The disillusionment with the faith was not hard to understand. For over four centuries it had been official theology that God had made a covenant with David whereby his dynasty would occupy the throne forever, with the Divine Presence permanently located in the Temple of Jerusalem. Now the dynasty had been wiped out with the throne, the Temple had been destroyed with the kingdom, and the people were in exile or living in the land under an alien heel. What was left as an anchor, as a basis for future hopes? It is remarkable that this small crushed nation, bereft of state and sanctuary, did not fade out of history, as the other nations round it would do. What preserved it was that its prophets and sages had constructed a kingdom of the spirit that could be carried into captivity when the political kingdom had gone.

13

The Kingdom of the Spirit

The story of the Hebrew kingship is woven into the story of the Hebrew faith. While one struggled against human foes, the other struggled against their heathen gods.

After the climactic moment on Mount Sinai, the austere Mosaic creed brought over the desert to the Promised Land started to be contaminated even before the Children of Israel had crossed the river Jordan. Later, as they settled on the soil, during the period of the Judges, there was a ceaseless battle against the seductive Canaanite nature-cults that seeped in at every hill-top shrine. The Israelite peasants and shepherds adjusted to the same agricultural seasons as their neighbours, and faced the same elements. It was hard for them to resist the fertility rites that promised good harvests and many lambs; or the ancient ceremonies thought to spur the coming of the first rains. The problem was not apostasy, a conscious switch from one deity to another, but rather the blurring of the borders between them.

During the monarchy the erosion took place not only at the rural grass-roots level, but also among the richer and more cosmopolitan classes that sprang up in the cities. Israelite courtiers, merchants, landowners and intellectuals mingled with foreigners from Egypt, Phoenicia, Assyria and Babylon and absorbed some of their culture and cults. Sometimes these influences were brought in by the foreign wives of Hebrew kings, such as Solomon's harem in Jerusalem or Queen Jezebel in Ahab's Samaria.

David, the architect of Hebrew statehood, combined brilliant political instincts with a devout heart. For him the kingdom and the faith were bound up with one another, and Jerusalem, 'David's city', was their common centre. His son Solomon translated this concept into gleaming stone. Side by side on Mount Moriah stood the Temple and the palace. In the one the Divine Presence hovered over the Ark recovered by David and brought by him to Jerusalem. In the other was enthroned the dynasty consecrated for all time by God's covenant with David. It was believed that the fusion of 'Church and State', of the secular and ecclesiastical powers, under divine protection would preserve the Hebrew identity and ensure its future.

This unique alliance of a dynasty, a sanctuary and a city within the framework of a united kingdom, could be called the establishment formula for survival. It received a body-blow when the kingdom split, and the northern tribes (the majority of the nation) rejected David's throne, Solomon's Temple and the Jerusalem capital. On that parting of the ways, the biblical writers had no doubt where they stood. For them the secessionist northern kingdom of Israel never acquired legitimacy, and the original sin of Jeroboam, the son of Nebat, was visited upon all his successors.

After the break, on the shrunken stage of Judah, the Davidic design – the kingdom, the dynasty, the Temple and the city – remained intact through all the ups and downs of the three and a half centuries it lasted. The glittering Temple, with its elaborate priesthood and rituals, and the countrywide pilgrimages to it on the three annual festivals, maintained a prestige that the rival shrines in the northern kingdom at Bethel and Dan could not share. But the fight against pagan infiltration depended in the first instance on the personality and outlook of each occupant of the throne. Of the twenty kings of Judah after the monarchy split, all but six are condemned by the Bible for religious and moral laxity and the heathen practices they permitted. The exceptions are Asa, Jehoshaphat and Jehoash in the ninth century BC, Uzziah and Hezekiah in the eighth, and Josiah in the seventh. In varying degrees they attempted to restore the moral health of the kingdom by purifying and repairing the Temple, destroying pagan altars and images, driving out idolatrous priests, and reviving observance of the festivals. Both Hezekiah and Josiah launched a drive to close down the local shrines and to concentrate religious observance exclusively in the Temple. Both of them also tried to draw back into the fold the remnants of the northern tribes after the kingdom of Israel had been smashed by Assyria.

The reformer kings in Judah represented the recurrent impulse to purge the established order from within. This process became stronger after the northern kingdom had been wiped out and the southern kingdom was battling to survive.

Two other developments were taking place in these centuries that were to make the Hebrew faith and identity independent of the established order and enable them to outlive the kingdom. One was the moulding of the Old Testament; the other was the classical prophetic movement. Both were to be of profound and enduring importance in the spiritual history of mankind.

THE BIBLE TAKES SHAPE

It is a strange thought that the greatest 'best seller' ever known was compiled by scholars, scribes and editors about whom nothing is known, not even their names. The Old Testament is not a book. It is an anthology of Hebrew sacred literature shaped over a thousand years, and containing legal codes, historical narratives, sermons, legends and folktales, prophecies, proverbs and poetry. The little Hebrew hill-nation had a superb gift for telling its own story. By word of mouth, from father to son, the Israelites related the wanderings of their patriarchal ancestors, their liberation from slavery, the commandments handed down to them in thunder and lightning, the deeds of their kings and warriors, and the wisdom of their prophets. They were much buffeted by the imperial powers of the time; but in the end the pen was mightier than the sword, and the faith outlived the empires. Abraham, Moses and Isaiah loom more majestically through the mists of time than Rameses or Nebuchadnezzar. Ruth the Moabite girl is more familiar to us than the glittering queens of Nineveh, Babylon and Thebes who have passed on to dusty oblivion.

The task of collecting and editing the mass of oral traditions and written annals started independently in the two kingdoms of Israel and Judah, after the monarchy had split. The earliest version of the Books of Moses, or the *Torah* (a Hebrew word that means 'teaching', though it is usually referred to as the 'Law'), was compiled in Judah about the middle of the ninth century BC. It is known to Bible scholars by the letter 'J', since in it the Lord is known as Jehovah (Yahweh). A century later a parallel version appeared in the northern kingdom of Israel; it is labelled 'E', since it used for the Deity the name Elohim, derived from the Canaanite *El*. At some time in the seventh century, the two were woven together into a single compilation that the scholars call JE.

The 'Book of the Law', found in the Temple about 622 BC in the reign of King Josiah, is regarded as having been an early version of the Deuteronomic Code. That Book, as it exists today, is in the form of three addresses by Moses to the Children of Israel before they entered the Promised Land. In substance the Book is a reaffirmation of the Sinai Covenant and a revision of the earlier laws (particularly the code of the covenant in Exodus 23) in the light of the six centuries that had passed since Moses. The Deuteronomic Code reflects a settled agricultural economy, the growth of urban life, private ownership of land and other forms of property, and the evolution of political institutions and social classes. The Hebrew society of the seventh century BC had come a long way from its nomad ancestors who lived off their cattle and sheep under the authority of their tribal elders.

The religious and legal concepts in the Deuteronomic Code were influenced not only by changed conditions of life, but also by the lofty ethical ideas, social concern and humanism of the classical prophets – especially Isaiah, who had died some two generations before the Book of Deuteronomy came to light in the Temple. The identity of the Book's author is conjectural; he may have been a priest in the Jerusalem Temple, or, according to another theory, a learned preacher among the northern tribes.

By the time the first Temple period of Jewish history came to an end with the destruction of Jerusalem in 587 BC, the Torah had already taken shape as a group of five Books attributed to Moses: Genesis, Exodus, Leviticus, Numbers and Deuteronomy. In the western world they became known as the *Pentateuch*, a Greek word meaning 'five scrolls'. In addition, early texts were extant of the historical Books of Joshua, Judges, Samuel and Kings, as well as the recorded utterances of the classical prophets from Amos to Jeremiah. The most important part of the Old Testament was therefore carried into the Babylonian exile.

The work of compiling and revising was to go on for a further six or seven centuries. In Babylonia a group of priests produced another strand known to Bible students as the Priestly Code, with the symbol 'P'. Probably as a reaction to the outlook of the prophets and the broad spirit of Deuteronomy, the Priestly Code stressed the organized and formal side of religion. It dealt with the functions of the priests and Levites and gave precise directions for sacrifices, festivals and purification rituals. Writing at a time when the Temple had ceased to exist, the authors showed their faith in its reconstruction, and wanted to preserve every detail about it for the future. The 'P' layer was in due course incorporated into the text of the Books of Moses, especially the latter part of Exodus and Leviticus. The name of Ezra the Scribe is associated with this Code, and it was probably the basic element in the 'book of the law of God', also referred to as 'the book of the law of Moses', that Ezra brought with him to Jerusalem after the Return, and read out to the people.

Some time in the fourth century BC, between a hundred and fifty to two hundred years after the Return and the beginning of the Second Temple, the Book of Chronicles appeared. (Originally written on a single scroll Chronicles, like Samuel and Kings, was divided very much later into two books for convenient handling.) After a brief résumé from Genesis onward in the form of genealogical tables the anonymous Chronicler retells the history of the monarchy from Saul to the fall of Jerusalem and the Babylonian exile. This is ground already covered by the Books of Samuel and Kings. Parts of those texts are repeated in Chronicles, other parts are omitted, amplified or changed to suit the Chronicler's purpose and the needs of his own time. Judah was then a small and obscure province of the Persian empire, with the modest, rebuilt Temple as its central institution. David is presented as the ideal king, with great credit given to him as a fount of Temple liturgy and music and levitical functions, in which the Chronicler has an absorbing interest. The Book has such an overriding attachment to Jerusalem, the Temple and the Davidic dynasty that the history of the northern kingdom of Israel is virtually ignored.

The Book of Chronicles continues straight into the Books of Ezra and Nehemiah that tell the story of the Return. They are regarded as also having been edited by the same Chronicler, as part of a single large work. It is not surprising that biblical Books compiled and rewritten by many hands, from varying sources, and over many centuries, should contain the repetitions and discrepancies that preoccupy modern biblical scholars. However, one great unifying theme runs throughout: the story of a single small nation, told in the light of its covenant with God.

It was not until about 100 AD that the canon (authorized selection) of the Old Testament Books was settled by the rabbis at Javneh in the coastal plain, together with their division into three groups: the Law, the Prophets and the Writings. History had tragically repeated itself.

Jerusalem and the Second Temple had been destroyed in 70 AD – this time by the Roman legions – and the Second Jewish Commonwealth had ended in blood and flames. But by then the Land of Israel had become the Land of the Bible and the dispersed Hebrew nation had become the People of the Book. In that kingdom of the spirit it would survive for the next two thousand years.

THE PROPHETIC MOVEMENT

Hebrew prophecy rested on the belief that God's will was made known to his people through individuals chosen by him for the purpose. The Hebrew word for prophet, *navi*, denotes one who is 'called'. The call came to men of diverse characters and background: Moses, brought up as a prince in Pharaoh's household; Samuel, the young novice in the Shiloh sanctuary; royal chaplains like Nathan and Gad; Amos tending his sheep in the Hebron hills; Elisha behind his father's plough in the Jordan valley; and Isaiah the statesman and confidant of kings. Nor were women excluded from the prophetic vocation; it touched Miriam, the sister of Moses and Aaron; Deborah, who rallied the tribes in the period of the Judges; and Hulda, the seventh-century Jerusalem house-wife who was consulted by king Josiah. At the folk level the prophetic spirit could be collective, seizing upon bands and communes of mystics who worked themselves into religious ecstasy with the help of music and dancing. Saul was swept up by a group of 'sons of the prophets' after he had been privately anointed by Samuel.

To be God's mouthpiece and serve as the moral conscience of the community was a heavy burden. Those who received the call sometimes felt inadequate and shrank from their mission. When God's voice came to him from the burning bush, Moses pleaded a speech defect. Isaiah cried out: 'I am lost; for I am a man of unclean lips . . .' (Isaiah 6:5) Told to go on a prophetic journey to Nineveh, Jonah simply ran away to sea. Behind his combative manner Jeremiah was a sensitive man, torn by inner conflict, and suffering keenly from the hostility and ridicule he aroused: 'Woe is me, my mother, that you bore me, a man of strife and contention to the whole land . . . all of them curse me.' (Jeremiah 15:10)

Once the vocation was accepted, the prophets were utterly fearless and independent in carrying out their mission. Serving a higher master they did not hesitate to rebuke kings, clash with the priesthood, champion the poor and dispossessed, and utter opinions and predictions that aroused general fury.

In the Hebrew canon of the Old Testament, the Books of Joshua, Judges, Samuel and Kings are grouped together as the Former Prophets. They bring the prophetic story up to Elijah and Elisha in the ninth century BC. In the middle of the eighth century BC, Amos was the first of the unique line of Latter Prophets that for over three centuries was to accompany the history of the divided kingdoms, the Exile and the Return. They are also known as the Classical Prophets and as the Literary Prophets – because their message was written down either by themselves or their followers. Of the fifteen whose works (or fragments thereof) have survived, three – Isaiah, Jeremiah and Ezekiel – are singled out 'as major prophets' because of the length and scope of their separate Books. The others, known as 'minor prophets' because of the brevity of their works, are brought together in the Hebrew Old Testament in a single Book of The Twelve.

Amos first appeared in the kingdom of Israel about thirty years before its end. He was closely followed by Hosea. In the kingdom of Judah the half century of Isaiah's career spanned the reign of three kings. His younger contemporary was Micah. More than a century later Jeremiah lived through the death-throes of Judah. Minor prophets of the same period in Judah were Zephaniah, Nahum and Habakkuk.

After the destruction of Jerusalem in 587 BC, two of the greatest of all the prophets emerged in the Babylonian exile: Ezekiel (who had been deported from Jerusalem to Babylon with King Jehoiachin ten years before the destruction); and the anonymous author of the latter half of the Book of Isaiah, simply known as Deutero-Isaiah (the Second Isaiah).

Haggai and Zechariah were the prophets of the Return, and their pressure speeded up the rebuilding of the Temple in Jerusalem. After that the classical age of prophecy dies away in the Persian period with Malachi, Obadiah, Joel and Jonah.

In language of matchless beauty and vigour the classical prophets gave a new depth to Hebrew life and faith. With them, the major emphasis shifts from the fight against idolatry to the cry for a just society and a personal ethic. True faith, they insist, starts not on the sacrificial altar but in the heart of man, and in concern for one's fellowmen. Amos, the pioneer of the classical school, declares that the Lord does not delight in festivals and sacrifices, but demands of his people:

> Hate evil, and love good,
> and establish justice in the gate. [Amos 5:15]

He is echoed by Isaiah:

> What to me is the multitude of your sacrifices?
> says the Lord;
> I have had enough of burnt offerings of rams
> and the fat of fed beasts;
> I do not delight in the blood of bulls,
> or of lambs, or of he-goats . . .
> cease to do evil.
> learn to do good;
> seek justice,
> correct oppression;
> defend the fatherless,
> plead for the widow. [Isaiah 1:11, 16, 17]

What does the Lord require of a man, asks Micah:

> But to do justice, and to love kindness,
> and to walk humbly with your God? [Micah 6:8]

Jeremiah thunders at the crowd of worshippers in the Temple courtyard that the Lord rejected their worship without morality:

'Will you steal, murder, commit adultery, swear falsely, burn incense to Baal . . . and then come and stand before me in this house, which is called by my name, and say, "We are delivered!" – only to go on doing all these abominations?' (Jeremiah 7: 9, 10)

The prophets were deeply involved in contemporary events. They were not political revolutionaries; their aim was to purge the institutions of the kingdom, not to overthrow them. Their stinging oracles against external foes place them among the great masters in the literature of invective – but this patriotism carried with it no indulgence on the home front. Dangerous foreign powers were, for the prophets, only the instruments of God's displeasure. If the rulers and people walked in his ways, they would be safe; if not, they would go under. No weapons or military pacts could avert that dread decree. The message became sharper in Isaiah's time, after the fall of Samaria and the reduction of Judah to a helpless Assyrian satellite.

Isaiah and Jeremiah boldly questioned the official doctrine of David's covenant with God, and went back to the spirit of the earlier Sinai covenant. Divine protection could never be taken for granted; it had to be earned by obedience, religious purity and just conduct. Unless the kingdom of Judah reformed itself, it too could be swept away, and with it the Davidic dynasty. Jeremiah was nearly killed by the crowd in the Temple courtyard for declaring that even God's sanctuary was not immune from destruction.

By these courageous attitudes the prophets tried to avert calamity – or prepare the nation for it if it came. The pessimism of their predictions was tempered by Messianic hopes for the future. It was not God's design that his erring people should be wiped out and disappear. Amos had already promised in the eighth century BC that there would be a national rebirth after the coming destruction: 'I will restore the fortunes of my people Israel, and they shall rebuild the ruined cities and inhabit them . . . and they shall never again be plucked up out of the land which I have given them.' (Amos 9:14, 15) In Isaiah's dazzling vision a 'remnant' would be saved and returned to Zion, there to live in a kingdom of peace and righteousness. With that prospect Ezekiel and the Second Isaiah consoled the exiles, whose pain and longing found such poignant expressions in Psalm 137, starting: 'By the waters of Babylon, there we sat down and wept, when we remembered Zion.'

Ezekiel, the strangest and most complex of the prophets, probably served as a priest in the Temple before being taken off to Babylonia in the first deportation of 598 BC. The latter half of his Book depicts in great detail the Temple standing again in Jerusalem, and the Hebrew nation restored to its kingdom under a ruler of David's line. The powerful symbol of resurrection in Ezekiel is the valley of dry bones stirring to new life.

The section of the Book of Isaiah attributed to the Second Isaiah opens with the words:

> Comfort, comfort my people
> says your God.
> Speak tenderly to Jerusalem,
> and cry to her
> that her warfare is ended,
> that her iniquity is pardoned,
> that she has received from the
> Lord's hand
> double for all her sins. [Isaiah 40:1, 2]

The passage was written at a time when Cyrus, the enlightened king of Persia, had conquered Babylonia and was emerging as the new master of the Near East. The Second Isaiah hails Cyrus as the divine instrument for Jewish redemption. The prophetic message is now universal in its scope. God had elected his people to be a prophet-nation, a 'suffering servant'. The return of the Jews to their homeland would usher in a new world order, in which the monotheistic God of the Hebrew faith would be accepted as the Lord of all creation.

Chronology

BC	ISRAELITE	GENERAL
1250	*THE EXODUS AND THE CONQUEST*	
		Rameses II: 1290–1224
	The Exodus *c.* 1250 The Law at Mount Sinai	
		Egypt loses control of Canaan
	Joshua's conquest of Canaan *c.* 1220–1200	
		End of Hittite Empire
1200	*THE JUDGES* Settlement of tribal areas from about 1200 Wars of: Ehud	
		Philistines settle in southern coastal area of Canaan
	Shamgar	
1150		

	Deborah
	    Gideon
	    Jephthah
		Eclipse of Egyptian Empire

1100		
	Exploits of Samson Migration of the tribe of Dan	
		Rise of Aramean kingdoms: Aram-Damascus, Zobah, Hamath
1050	Philistine victory at Aphek Destruction of Shiloh Era of Samuel	Philistine domination of western Canaan

BC	ISRAELITE		GENERAL

THE UNITED MONARCHY
(*1020–922*)
Saul: 1020–1000
   Philistine victory at Mount Gilboa and
   death of Saul

1000 *David*: 1000–961
   Capture of Jerusalem
   Expansion of Israelite Empire
   Ark of the Law brought to Jerusalem
   Revolt of Absalom

   Solomon: 961–922
950   Building of Temple
   Red Sea trade route   Shishak (*c.* 935–914)
   Visit of Queen of Sheba   founds twenty-second
   Death of Solomon and division of   Egyptian Dynasty.
   kingdom 922   Rezon regains
                              independence for
                              Aram-Damascus

THE TWO KINGDOMS
(*922–587*)

	Judah (*922–587*)	Israel (*922–722*)	
	Rehoboam: 922–915	*Jeroboam*: 922–901	Shishak's campaign
	Abijah: 915–913	*Nadab*: 901–900	against the Hebrew
900	*Asa*: 913–873	*Baasha*: 900–877	kingdoms
	Jehoshaphat: 873–849	*Elah*: 877–876	
		Zimri: 876	
		Omri: 876–869	
		Founding of Samaria	
		Ahab: 869–850	Mesha king of Moab
			Assyrian Domination
			Campaigns of
		Elijah	Shalmaneser III:
			859–824
			Battle of Karkar 853
850		*Ahaziah*: 850–849	
	Jehoram: 849–842	*Jehoram*: 849–842	
		Elisha	
	Ahaziah: 842	*Jehu*: 842–815	
	Athaliah: 842–837		
	Jehoash: 837–800		Hazael, king of
		Jehoahaz: 815–801	Aram-Damascus.
			Adad-nirari III:
			811–783
800	*Amaziah*: 800–783	*Joash*: 801–786	
			Ben-hadad II, king of
			Aram-Damascus

156

BC	ISRAELITE		GENERAL
	Judah	Israel	
	Uzziah: 783–742	*Jeroboam II*: 786–746	
		Amos	
750		Hosea	Tiglath-pileser III: 745–727
		Zechariah: 746–745	
	Jotham: 742–735	*Shallum*: 745	
		Menahem: 745–738	
	Ahaz: 735–715	*Pekahiah*: 738–737	
	Isaiah	*Pekah*: 737–732	Shalmaneser V: 727–722
	Micah	*Hoshea*: 732–724	
		Fall of Samaria Deportations	Sargon II: 722–705
	Hezekiah: 715–687		
700			Sennacherib: 705–681 Invasion of Judah: 701
	Manasseh: 687–642		
			Esarhaddon: 681–669 Asshurbanipal: 669–633
650			
	Amon: 642–640		
	Josiah: 640–609		
	Religious reforms		Fall of Nineveh to Babylonians: 612
	Jehoahaz: 609		Battle of Megiddo: 609
	Jehoiakim: 609–598		Babylonian Domination
	Jeremiah		
600	*Jehoiachin*: 598		Nebuchadnezzar: 605–562
	First deportations to Babylonia		
	Ezekiel		
	Jerusalem surrenders		
	Zedekiah: 598–587		
	Fall of Jerusalem		
	Deportations to Babylonia		
	Judah a Babylonian province		
	Gedaliah assassinated		
	Babylonian Exile		
	Second Isaiah		
550			Persian Domination
	The Return		Fall of Babylon: 539
	Edict of Cyrus and beginning of the Return to Judah 538		Cyrus: 550–530

BC	ISRAELITE	GENERAL
	Zerubbabel	
	Temple rebuilt: 520–515	
	Haggai	
	Zechariah	

Note: In dating the reigns of the Hebrew kings, the author has followed the chronology of Professor W. F. Albright.

Maps

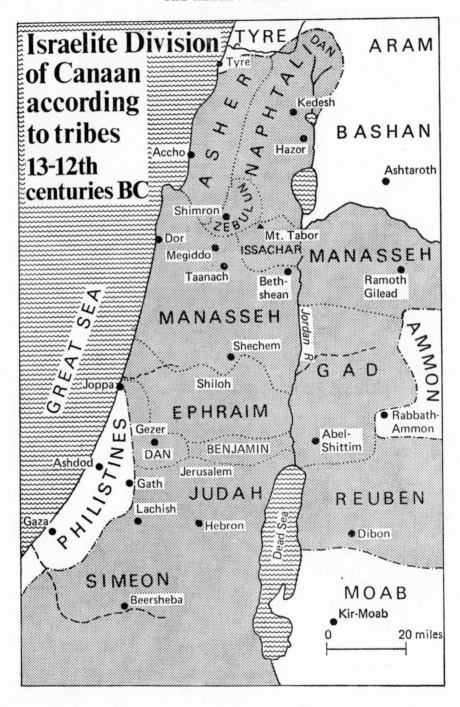

Israelite Division of Canaan according to tribes 13-12th centuries BC

TYRE

ARAM

DAN

Tyre

Kedesh

BASHAN

ASHER

NAPHTALI

Hazor

Accho

Ashtaroth

Shimron

ZEBULUN

Mt. Tabor

Dor

ISSACHAR

MANASSEH

Megiddo

Taanach

Beth-shean

Ramoth Gilead

GREAT SEA

MANASSEH

Jordan R.

Shechem

GAD

AMMON

Joppa

Shiloh

EPHRAIM

Gezer

Rabbath-Ammon

DAN

BENJAMIN

Abel-Shittim

Ashdod

Jerusalem

Gath

PHILISTINES

JUDAH

REUBEN

Gaza

Lachish

Hebron

Dead Sea

Dibon

SIMEON

MOAB

Beersheba

Kir-Moab

0   20 miles

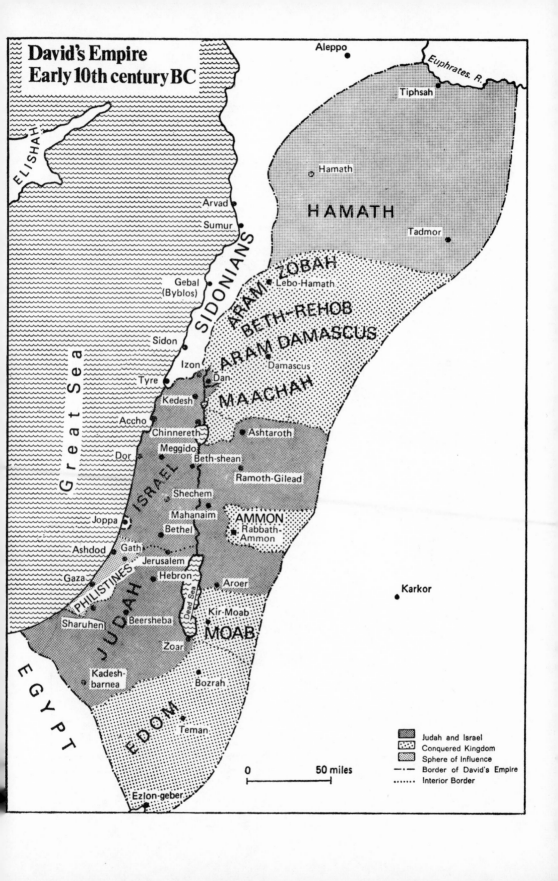

**David's Empire
Early 10th century BC**

Aleppo

Euphrates. R.

Tiphsah

ELISHAH

Hamath

HAMATH

Arvad

Tadmor

Sumur

SIDONIANS

ARAM-ZOBAH

Gebal
(Byblos)

Lebo-Hamath

BETH-REHOB

ARAM DAMASCUS

Sidon

Izon

Damascus

Tyre

Dan

MAACHAH

Kedesh

Accho

Ashtaroth

Chinnereth

Meggido

Beth-shean

Great Sea

Dor

ISRAEL

Ramoth-Gilead

Shechem

Joppa

Mahanaim

AMMON

Bethel

Rabbath-
Ammon

Ashdod

Gath

Jerusalem

PHILISTINES

Hebron

Gaza

Aroer

Karkor

JUDAH

Dead Sea

Sharuhen

Beersheba

Kir-Moab

MOAB

Zoar

Kadesh-
barnea

Bozrah

EGYPT

EDOM

Teman

	Judah and Israel
	Conquered Kingdom
	Sphere of Influence
–·–·–	Border of David's Empire
······	Interior Border

0   50 miles

Ezion-geber

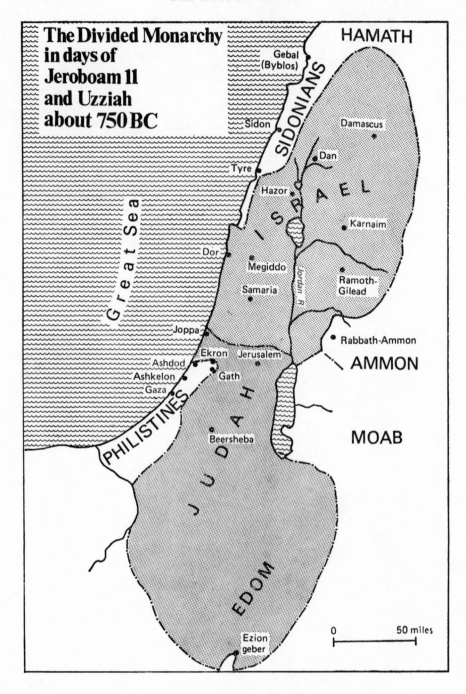

The Divided Monarchy
in days of
Jeroboam 11
and Uzziah
about 750 BC

HAMATH

Gebal
(Byblos)

SIDONIANS

Sidon

Damascus

Tyre

Dan

Hazor

ISRAEL

Karnaim

Great Sea

Dor

Megiddo

Jordan R.

Ramoth-
Gilead

Samaria

Joppa

Rabbath-Ammon

AMMON

Ekron

Jerusalem

Ashdod

Gath

Ashkelon

Gaza

PHILISTINES

JUDAH

MOAB

Beersheba

0   50 miles

EDOM

Ezion
geber

Index

Aaron, 82, 150
Abdon, 8
Abel-beth-maacah, 55
Abiathar, high priest, 25, 26, 45, 50, 56, 59
Abigail, sister of David, 53
Abigail, wife of David, 27, 47
Abijah, king of Judah, 78, 84
Abijah, son of Samuel, 3
Abimelech, 9–10
Abishag the Shunammite, 56, 59
Abishai, 28, 35, 42, 45, 51, 53, 54, 55
Abner, 28, 34–5, 36, 45, 52, 57, 96
Abraham, 80, 147
Absalom, 35, 45, 47, 48–54, 55, 58, 68
Achish, king of Gath, 25, 28–30, 38
Adad-nariri III, king of Assyria, 110, 115
Adam ford, 52
Adamah, ford of, 93
Adonijah, 56–7, 58, 59, 68
Adoniram, 45
Adoram, 76
Adullam, 26, 46
Africa, 62
Agag, king of the Amalekites, 18
Ahab, king of Israel, 81, 86, 89–102, 103, 104, 109
Ahaz, king of Judah, 118, 120, 122, 123, 125, 126, 132
Ahaziah, king of Judah, 103–4, 107, 108, 109, 111
Ahijah, 70, 79, 83
Ahikam, 137, 143
Ahimaaz, 50, 53, 58
Ahimelech, 25
Ahinoam, 27, 47
Ahithophel, 45, 49, 50, 51, 52
Ain Harod spring, 9
Ajalon, vale of, 17
Albright, W. F., 69
Allenby, General, 67
Amalekites, 18, 19, 29, 32–3
Amariah, high priest, 88
Amasa, 53, 55, 57
Amaziah, king of Judah, 111, 112–14, 115
Amaziah, priest, 117
Ammon, Ammonites, 7, 10, 139; Saul's campaign against, 18; war with Israel, 41–3; regains independence, 83; invasion of Judah, 86; becomes vassal state of Judah, 118, 120; and Assyria, 122; and revolt against Babylon, 140–1
Amnon, 47–8, 58
Amon, king of Judah, 132
Amorites, 7
Amos, prophet, 116–17, 148, 150, 151–2, 153
Anath, 9
Anathoth, 59, 137
Anatolia, 8
Aphek, 10, 29, 32, 93
Apis, 82
Arabia, 61, 62, 63, 87, 118, 121, 124
Arad, 78, 113, 141
Aram-Damascus (Syria), 7; and Israel's war with Ammon, 42; wars with Israel, 41, 84–5, 86, 92–3, 100–2, 105–6, 107, 110–11, 112; relationship with Israel, 61, 75, 89, 90–1; regains independence, 71, 83; and Assyria, 94, 110, 115, 121, 122, 123; Israel's suzerainty over, 115; Egypt tries to gain control over, 135
Arameans, 42
Araunah the Jebusite, 46, 64
Aravah valley, 63, 78, 113
Ark of the Covenant (Ark of the Law): Philistines capture, 29, 39; David and, 39–40, 44, 46–7, 50, 146; at Bethel, 80; in Solomon's Temple, 65, 66
Armageddon, 67
Aroer, 46
Asa, king of Judah, 84–6, 87, 89–90, 146
Asahel, 34–5
Asahel, 45
Ashdod, 7, 39, 41, 118, 127
Asher, tribe of, 6, 9
Ashkelon, 7, 41, 122, 128, 136
Ashtaroth, 123
Asia Minor, 61
Asshur, 134
Asshurbanipal, king of Assyria, 131, 134
Asshur-nasir-pal III, king of Assyria, 94
Assyria, 4, 8, 93–5, 96, 136; domination of Judah, 15, 121, 125; captures Samaria, 75, 91; threat to Israel, 109–10, 121–4;

163

Index

and Assyria, 110, 122, 127; and revolt against Babylon, 140
Eglon, king of Moab, 9
Egypt, 4, 93, 143; Philistines attack coast of, 7; and circumcision, 24; Solomon and, 60–1, 69; wars with Israel and Judah, 67, 76, 77–8; trade routes, 90; and Assyria, 127, 128, 131, 134, 135; Judah a vassal of, 136; war with Babylonians, 138, 139, 141–2
Ehud, 9
Eilat, 63
Ekron, 7, 39, 41, 128
Elah, king of Israel, 89
Elah, vale of, 21, 22
Eli, high priest, 10–11, 25
Eliakim, 129
Eliam, 45
Eliav, 22
Elijah the Tishbite, prophet, 92, 79–100, 103, 105, 107, 108, 151
Elisha, prophet, 100, 104, 106, 107, 110–11, 150, 151
Elon, 8
En-dor, 30
En-gedi, 28, 86, 141
En-rogel, 56–7
Ephraim, territory of, 8, 11, 48, 77, 90, 110; tribe of, 4, 5, 6, 9, 10, 53, 70, 79, 84
Esarhaddon, king of Assyria, 131
Ethbaal, king of Sidon, 90
Ethiopia, Ethiopians, 64, 85
Euphrates river, 136
Ezekiel, prophet, 151, 153
Ezion-geber (Eilat), 62–3, 78, 87, 103, 106, 118, 119, 122
Ezra the Scribe, 149

First World War, 93

Gad, 45, 46, 150
Gad, tribe of, 6, 9
Galilee, 6, 9, 66, 75, 90, 110, 122
Gath, 7, 21, 25, 39, 41, 45, 59, 110, 112, 118
Gaza, 7, 10, 41, 78, 120, 122
Geba, 16, 17
Geber, 85
Gedaliah, governor, 142–3
Gerar, 85
Gerizim, Mount, 10
Geruth Chimham, 143
Geshur, 7, 47, 48
Gezer, 6, 60–1, 66–7, 68, 77, 78
Gibbethon, 84, 89
Gibeah, 11, 15, 16
Gibeon, 34, 60
Gibeon, pool of, 96
Gibeonites, 36–7
Gideon, 4, 9
Gihon, spring of, 38, 57, 96, 127, 129
Gilboa, Mount, 29, 30, 31, 33
Gilead, 6, 8, 9, 10, 34, 52, 84, 90, 97
Gilgal, 13, 14, 16, 19, 54, 55
Giloh, 52

Gittites, 45
Golan Heights, 47
golden calves, 81–2
Goliath, 21–2, 25
Gozan, 123–4
Greece, 62
Gulf of Aqaba, 61

Habakkuk, prophet, 151
Habor river, 123–4
Hadad, 70
Hadad-ezer, king of Zobah, 42
Haggai, prophet, 151
Haifa, 67
Haile Selassie, emperor of Ethiopia, 64
Hamath, 42, 115, 121, 124
Hananiah, 119
Hanun, king of the Ammonites, 42, 52–3
Haran, 134
Hazael, king of Aram-Damascus, 107, 109, 110, 111, 112
Hazor, 66–7, 68, 77, 95, 96, 116, 122–3
Hebron, 34, 35, 36, 49, 57, 113
Hebron hills, 6, 26, 86
Helam, battle of, 42
Hermon, Mount, 81
Herod the Great, king of Judah, 71, 91
Hezekiah, king of Judah, 96, 125–31, 132, 133, 146
Hilkiah, high priest, 133
Hinnom valley, 40, 132, 134
Hiram, king of Tyre, 41, 61, 62, 64, 65
Hittites, 4, 7, 8, 93
Hophra, Pharaoh, 141
Hosea, prophet, 117, 151
Hoshaiah, 141
Hoshea, king of Israel, 123
Hula, 90
Huldah, prophetess, 133, 150
Hurvat Uzza, 119
Hushai the Archite, 50, 51–2
Hussein, king of Jordan, 15

Ibzan, 8
Isaiah, prophet, 126, 137, 147, 150–3; on Samaria, 91; and Assyrian threat, 127, 128, 130–1, 138
Ishbosheth, 34, 35, 36, 52
Israel: wars with Philistines, 3, 14, 16–17, 21–2, 29–31, 33–4, 41; tribes, 4–6; conquest of Canaan, 5; technological advances, 5–6; prophets, 12–13, 150–4; civil war with Judah, 35, 36; capture of Jerusalem, 37–8; war with Ammonites, 41–3; army in David's reign, 45–6; expansion under David, 61; trade with Phoenicia, 62–3; wars with Canaan, 68; population, 69; reform under Solomon, 69–70; as a separate kingdom, 75–6, 77, 79–85, 86, 89–92; Egyptian campaign, 77–8; wars with Aram-Damascus, 92–3, 100–2, 105–6, 107, 110–11, 112; and Assyria, 94–5, 109–10, 121–4; relationship with Phoenicia, 96–7, 109, 116,

165

Index

68; destroyed by Pharaoh Shishak, 78, 95; rebuilt by Ahab, 95–6; destroyed by Assyrians, 122–3

Melkart, god, 97

Memphis, 82, 131

Menahem, king of Israel, 121–2

Menelik, 64

Mephibosheth, 36, 50, 54

Merab, 23, 37

Mesha, king of Moab, 90, 104, 105

Mesha Stele, 90

Mesopotamia, 7, 8, 29, 61, 67, 94, 128, 135, 136

Micah, prophet, 81, 151, 152

Micaiah, 101

Michal, 23–4, 27, 35, 40

Michmash, 16, 17

Midianites, 9

Miriam, prophetess, 150

Mizpah, 11, 13, 14, 85, 142, 143

Moab, 7, 9; Saul's campaign against, 18; Israel conquers, 43, 83, 89, 90; invasion of Judah, 86; Jehoram of Israel wages war against, 104–5; and Assyria, 122, 127; and Babylon, 139, 140

Moreh hill, 29

Moriah, Mount, 41, 46, 64, 146

Mosaic Code, 81–2, 145

Moses, prophet, 4, 40, 71, 80, 82, 147, 148, 150

Naamah, 76

Nabal, 26–7

Nabateans, 113

Nablus, 93

Naboth's vineyard, 100, 108

Nadab, king of Israel, 84

Nahash, king of Ammon, 13

Nahum, prophet, 135, 151

Naphtali, tribe of, 6, 9

Napoleon, emperor of the French, 67

Nathan, 44, 45, 46–7, 57, 150

Nebuchadnezzar II, king of Babylon, 136, 138, 139–40, 141, 142, 143

Nebuzaradan, 142

Neco, Pharaoh, 135, 136

Negev, 6, 18, 78, 87, 90, 106, 113, 119

Nile valley, 7, 29, 61

Nineveh, 94, 129, 132, 134, 136, 150

Nob, 25, 26

Obadiah, prophet, 98, 151

Olives, Mount of, 50

Omri, king of Israel, 89–92, 95, 104, 109

Ophel spur, 40

Ophir, 62, 64, 87

Osorkon I, Pharaoh, 85

Othniel, 8–9

Padi, king of Ekron, 128

paganism, 97–9, 109, 111–12, 132, 146

Palestine, 135

Palti, 27, 35

Pekah, king of Israel, 122, 123, 126

Pekahiah, king of Israel, 122

Penuel, 84

Persia, 149, 151, 153

Philistia, Philistines, 7, 81, 85; wars with Israel, 3, 6, 10–11, 14, 16–17, 21–2, 29–31, 33–4, 41, 84; iron-smelting, 5; Ark of the Covenant captured by, 10–11, 39; and circumcision, 24; attempt to capture Jerusalem from David, 38–9; and David's army, 45; conquered by Egypt, 77; relationship with Judah, 87, 106, 118, 122; and Assyria, 110, 122, 128; Babylonian conquest of, 136

Phoenicia, Phoenicians, 7, 81; relationship with Israel, 41, 61, 62–3, 65, 69, 75, 89, 90, 91, 96–7, 109, 116; Assyrian invasion, 94, 122; pays tribute to Assyria, 121

Priestly Code, 148–9

prophetic movement, 150–4

Rabbath-ammon (Amman), 42, 43, 53, 96, 119

Rachel, 4, 19

Ramah, 3, 18, 28, 84, 85, 143

Ramat Rahel, 138

Rameses II, Pharaoh, 8

Ramoth-gilead, 86, 90, 101, 104, 107

Red Sea, 61, 62, 63, 64, 103, 106, 118

Rehoboam, king of Judah, 76, 77, 78, 79, 85

Remaliah, 122

Rephaim, vale of, 38

Reuben, tribe of, 6, 9

Rezin, king of Aram-Damascus, 122, 126

Rezom, king of Aram-Damascus, 71

Rhodes, 62

Riblah, 142

Rishon-le-Zion, 128

Rizpah, 35, 37

Roman empire, 62, 150

Ruth the Moabite, 19, 26, 147

Samaria, 108, 110; foundation of, 91–2, 95; Jehoshaphat visits, 101; besieged by Syria, 105–6; and Jeroboam II, 116; Assyria besieges, 75, 91, 123, 152

Samaria (province), 125, 134

Samaritans, 124

Samson the Danite, 10

Samuel, prophet, 3, 10–11, 28, 80, 150; and Saul, 12–18, 30; and David, 19–20, 24

Sardinia, 62

Sargon II, king of Assyria, 123, 124, 127, 128

Saul, king of Israel, 11, 12–18, 19–31, 33–4, 36–7, 45, 79, 150

Scopus, Mount, 25

Seir, Mount, 86

Sela (Petra), 113

Sennacherib, king of Assyria, 128–9, 130–1

Seruiah, 44–5

Shabaku, Pharaoh, 127